Gleanings from the New Testament

A. M. HUNTER

Gleanings from the New Testament

THE WESTMINSTER PRESS
PHILADELPHIA

Published in Great Britain under the title
Gospel and Apostle

Published by The Westminster Press®
Philadelphia, Pennsylvania

Printed in the United States of America

Library of Congress Cataloging in Publication Data

Hunter, Archibald Macbride.
  Gleanings from the New Testament.

  Includes bibliographical references and index.
  1. Bible. N.T.—Addresses, essays, lectures.
I. Title.
BS2395.H79 1975   225.6   75-33652
ISBN 0-664-24794-6

Contents

Preface

Here are thirty essays from the pen of a New Testament professor who, though now retired from Aberdeen, that grey city by the northern seas, still stays in love with his subject and, while his bow (hopefully) still abides in strength, would fain be an arrowy exponent of God's Word to men in Christ.

Very diverse are their themes: they range from the problem of faith and history and the importance of Greek grammar to the idea of a Christian gentleman and the relation between the apostolic preaching and the Apostles' Creed.

Four of the essays (22-25) have already appeared in *Life and Work*, the official record of the Church of Scotland. One (19) is due to appear in a forthcoming *Festschrift* for William Barclay. For permission to include these essays in my book I thank the editors of both these publications.

My warmest thanks for reading the proofs are again due to the Rev. David G. Gray (once of St Peter's, Dundee) with whom I now traverse, almost daily, 'the banks and braes o' bonnie Doon'.

Ayr 1975   A. M. Hunter

I

Revelation and Redemption

One of the things which exasperate Christians is the way in which 'the world' annexes and profanes the sacred words of the faith. The most recent victim is 'charisma' which for Paul meant a 'grace-gift' of God for use in the church and now describes any personal quality which enables a man to impress his fellows.[1] An earlier victim was the word 'revelation' now a name for a suitcase.

The dethroning of this 'numinous' word began when our liberal theologians last century took to equating it with discovery. For them, Christianity was 'the last and loftiest construction that man has put on the infinite' and the Christian idea of God the sublime discovery of that spiritual genius, Jesus of Nazareth, who by searching had found out God.

Yet even those who continue to equate 'revelation' with 'discovery' often suggest by their way of speaking that there is more to it than simple human seeking and finding. When they discover something unexpectedly, do they not exclaim, 'It came to me as a revelation'? In so saying, do they not unwittingly confess that what has been 'revealed' to them is something to which their passions or their obtuseness had previously made them blind? In such situations the question is whether the prime factor is man the seeker or whether God is not first personally active in removing the veil which blurs our spiritual vision. The latter, which is the biblical view, finds classical expression in Jesus' saying to Peter, 'Flesh and blood has not revealed this to you but my Father who is in heaven' (Matt. 16.17).

In origin, then, 'revelation' is a holy or 'numinous' word, and we ought only to employ it when we mean something which impinges on us from the beyond and which we try to interpret. In theistic terms, it is the self-disclosure of God or, in the fine phrase of Arthur Hallam, the friend of Tennyson, 'the voluntary approximation of the Infinite Being to the ways and thoughts of finite men'.

What kind of divine self-disclosure deserves the name of 'Christian revelation'? We answer, 'revelation is redemption'.

Avant garde Christians will dislike the retention of that *passé* and unpopular word 'redemption'. To them it suggests an outmoded evangelicalism, revivalist hymns of yester year, and a brand of pietistic Christianity unacceptable to those who cry out for 'religionless Christianity' and would have us name Christ not as the world's redeemer but as 'the man for others' *par excellence*. Surely, they will protest, we have learned to think of 'revelation' as something bigger and less *borné* than something which, to modern man, suggests only the pawn shop and the sign of the three golden balls. 'The heavens declare the glory of God and the firmament showeth his handiwork', says the Psalmist. Is there no divine revelation to be found in the created world around us? Was no revelation (however pantheistic it sounds) vouchsafed to William Wordsworth when he felt a presence which disturbed him with—

> a sense sublime
> Of something far more deeply interfused,
> Whose dwelling is the light of setting suns,
> And the round ocean and the living air,
> And the blue sky, and in the mind of man[2]?

Was there no divine revelation in the heroic self-sacrifice of a Captain Oates of Antarctic fame or a Maximilian Kolbe, the saint of Auschwitz?

To deny that God can and does reveal himself in such persons and places would be foolish. Moreover, even Paul whom we have quoted did not deny such a revelation – see Rom. 1.19f. The trouble is that (*a*) such a revelation can be very ambiguous (to some 'nature red in tooth and claw' has suggested something very different from divine revelation), and (*b*) such a revelation is so general as to be ineffectual for the mass of men. It does not assure us of God; it only suggests him. And it suggests God to certain individuals rather than to the world:

> ... Earth's crammed with heaven,
> And every common bush afire with God;
> But only he who sees takes off his shoes,
> The rest sit round it and pluck blackberries.[3]

The truth is that we are sinners, not sages; and what we need for our rescue is revelation given in history, in a person, and on a world scale, a revelation which brings not merely new light but new life – in short, regeneration.

Just such a revelation of God given in history, and through persons on a racial scale, is what the Bible claims to give. It is the record of God's dealings with a special people, Israel (whom he chose not for exclusive privilege but for universal witness and service – 'a light to lighten the Gentiles'), with prophets to interpret his ways to men, and it culminates in the coming of the man Christ Jesus (who is also the divine and unique Son of God), with apostles to interpret his finished work.

How is this revelation in history to be understood? The traditional way may be called *propositional*. The Bible is a compendium of divine truths, supernaturally and inerrantly communicated to men in the form of propositions from which we may construct a system of Christian belief. Yet how can human language ever adequately express the inexpressible – the majesty of the infinite God and his gracious condescension to us men in Christ? Moreover, if biblical criticism has taught us anything, it is that the Bible is not an arsenal of Christian evidences, neither does God save the world by authorship. What we have in the Bible is not an inerrant but a *sacramental* book, a book which, by the Holy Spirit's help, can yet mediate to men the historic grace of God in Christ.

Never perhaps was the matter better expressed than by William Robertson Smith when he stood arraigned for heresy: 'If I am asked why I accept the Bible as the Word of God, I answer with all the Fathers of the Protestant Church: because the Bible is the only record of the redeeming love of God, because in the Bible alone I find God drawing near to man in Christ Jesus and declaring to us, in him, his will for our salvation. And this record I know to be true by the witness of his Spirit in my heart whereby I am assured that none other than God himself can speak such words to my soul.'

A more modern way of conceiving Christian revelation may be called *pictorial*. We are to think of God as allowing himself to be seen in Christ or, perhaps, permitting himself to be explained. Proponents of this view find their proof-text in John 14.9. When Philip said to Jesus, 'Lord, show us the Father and we ask no more', he answered, 'Have I been all this time with you, Philip, and you still do not know me? Anyone who has seen me has seen the Father.' On this view, Christ came to show us the Father or, alternatively, to impart the truth about him. Either way, revelation is a kind of portrayal, and God's 'unspeakable gift' to men in Christ is a picture of himself to be admired or a truth about himself to be credited. But, attractive as it is to many modern Christians, this pictorial idea of revelation does not do justice to the main burden of the New Testament. It is one thing to say that in Christ God taught us the truth about himself, another to say that in Christ God himself came to seek and to save. It is one thing to say that a man on earth mirrors the glory of the invisible God, quite another to say that in that man God bowed the heavens and came down. And this is what the New Testament says. What God gave us in Christ was neither his portrait nor his principle but his own presence in saving action.

The true view of New Testament revelation is *personal and presential*. In Christ God gave us not his illuminating portrait but his saving presence. Or, to put the matter another way, in Christ God was his own apostle. Only such a redemptive revelation can match the need of sin-sick men. What we need is divine rescue, not divine reflection. And what we have in the New Testament is God in Christ giving himself in action, God meeting our sin with his grace – his extravagant love to undeserving men. Moreover, in the New Testament 'the cross and not the cradle holds the secret of the Lord'. The burning focus of revelation is not Bethlehem but Calvary. There God consummated his revelation in Christ, so that following Browning we can say:

> What lacks then of perfection fit for God
> But just the instance which this tale supplies
> Of love without a limit? So is strength,
> So is intelligence; let love be so,
> Unlimited in its self-sacrifice,
> Then is the tale true, and God shows complete.

It is a case of *per crucem ad lucem*, through the cross of light, light in the biblical sense,[4] light like the light which shone on Paul on the Damascus Road, saving light, light that not

only illumines but rescues and renews and regenerates – in
fine, redemption.

Such redemptive revelation we may compare to a tuning-
fork. God smote on the world in Christ's redeeming work;
it sounded in the apostles' 'word of reconciliation'; and it
reverberates, and goes on so doing, age after age, in the
Bible as the sacramental book.

There are thus three factors in New Testament revelation:
(1) God's historic action in Christ; (2) the apostles' inspired
interpretation of that act in their preaching (see I Cor. 2.11-
16) and (3) the Bible and the church's proclamation in
which, by the power of the Holy Spirit, the gospel of God's
grace prolongs itself and, in generation after generation,
becomes again 'the power of God unto salvation to every
man with faith'.

What then is 'the Word of God'? Not a Book ('the Word
incartulate' as A. C. Craig has called the 'fundamentalist'
view) but the God of all grace redemptively revealing himself to sinful men. This revelation is consummated in the
cross and its shining sequel. Christ is God's living Word in
whom he reconciles the world to himself. But the apostles'
preaching – their *kērygma* – is also the Word of God, because
through it the living Christ interprets his finished work to
men. And this Word, or gospel, prolongs itself today whenever and wherever the apostolic message is faithfully
preached and received.

In short, as it comes from God, the Word is Christ his Son;
as it comes from Christ, through the church, it is the apostles'
gospel as interpreted by the Holy Spirit; and the Bible itself
(which, like the church, was created by the gospel) becomes
the Word of God when, by the Spirit's power, it mediates
the historic grace of God to men.

NOTES

1. E.g., 'Onassis has that charisma which makes a man reach for his
camera.' *Sunday Telegraph*, 9 February 1975.

2. 'Lines Composed above Tintern Abbey'.

3. Elizabeth Barrett-Browning, 'Aurora Leigh', Bk vii.

4. For us, 'light' is the difference between knowledge and ignorance,
as it was for the Greeks. For the men of the Bible it is the difference
between security and danger. (Night-time is the time when wild beasts

prowl around and evil-doers go to work. Daytime is the time when men go about their lawful occasions in safety.) For us, 'light' has an intellectual nuance. For the Hebrew, it concerned living rather than thinking. 'The Lord is my light and my salvation' (Ps. 27.1). 'The people who walked in darkness have seen a great light' (Isa. 9.2). 'Arise, shine; for your light has come' (Isa. 60.1) etc. It is a figure for divine deliverance.

2

Faith and History

I

The Christian can never agree with Henry Ford that 'history is bunk'. Ours is a historical religion. Christian theology is an interpretation of history. What we call 'revelation' is God's self-disclosure in historical events. But when we use the word 'history', what sort do we have in mind? And what should be the relation of faith to it?

Such questions have deeply exercised our twentieth-century theologians – Karl Barth, Emil Brunner, Reinhold Niebuhr, C. H. Dodd, Oscar Cullmann, Alan Richardson, Wolfhart Pannenberg, and many another. Still today the relation of faith to history forms the subject of keen debate; but at long last we may see signs that our theologians are on the right track and making good progress.

The debate really began last century with the rise of the so-called 'scientific' or 'positivist' doctrine of history. This is the view that the only history with a claim to truth is that which can be verified by scientific method of the sort practised in the physical sciences. Last century's 'scientific' historians therefore saw their task as the re-discovery of the hard facts on the basis of which they could then proceed to generalize. They believed that an event and its interpretation could be successfully separated and that, stripping off the husk of interpretation, they could use the resultant kernel for their work of writing history.

With this concept of history Barth, Brunner and Bultmann found themselves fated to wrestle. They soon ran into trouble. For God and his action in history is a hypothesis of which the critical secular historian feels no need. (There is, we are bound to add, no *scientific* presupposition of the historical method which requires the historian to rule out the possibility of divine action in history, such as God's raising of Jesus from the dead.) So our three theologians proceeded to disengage themselves from history.

Barth and Brunner postulated a special kind of 'sacred history', a supra history beyond the arrows' range of the critical historians where the Christian faithful could cease from the critics' troubling and be at rest.

Bultmann took a different line. For him, there were two kinds of history: (1) *Historie*, the recounting of the bare facts, and (2) *Geschichte*, history interpreted in its (existential) significance for us. But for the incorrigibly sceptical Bultmann *Historie* was an impossible emprise because the gospels were palimpsests in which the faith of the early church had been so heavily written over the tradition about Jesus that now we can know next to nothing about him. So he focused on *Geschichte*, especially the apostles' *kērygma* which, after some 'demythologizing', he reinterpreted in terms of existentialism, the popular philosophy of the day, or, more precisely, the difficult and doubtfully theistic brand of it expounded by Martin Heidegger, his Marburg colleague.

All three theologians had escaped from what the mass of men mean by history – two into supra history, and one into a dubious existentialism. You might say that much of the malaise from which recent Christian theology suffered has been a 'hangover' from nineteenth-century 'positivist history'.

Meanwhile our secular historians had been changing their views about history and historiography. The old 'positivist' view they had now largely abandoned. There are no such things, they said, as bare facts. We cannot separate events from their interpretation. What we have to work with are interpreted events. And in dealing with such an event the only true critical way is to frame hypotheses and then test them by critical methods in order to find which one best fits the available evidence.

Yet this was only half of their new doctrine. History, they went on to add, is a two-way traffic between present and past. The past ceases to have meaning unless it is re-lived in the experience of each succeeding generation. The historian who is not involved in the history of his own time will never bring the past to life. His business is, in fact, to re-enact that past in his own mind by re-thinking it and so discovering its truth for himself.

It is this approach to history which our most recent theologians have been making their own. In 1964 there appeared two books, one in England and the other in Germany, which showed how our theologians had begun to profit from the new concept of historiography.

II

The English book was Alan Richardson's *History Sacred and Profane* (SCM Press 1964). For Richardson the field of divine self-disclosure is not some supra history but actual 'profane' history. Not the Greeks but the Hebrews were the true fathers of history. Whereas the Greeks regarded the historical process as but one of the rhythms of nature, the Hebrews, with their strong sense of history and their faith in the living God, expected disclosure situations – *'revelations'* – in the course of events. In the great crises of their nation's history they discerned the hand of the God who acts and whose workshop is history. What happened, for instance, at the Red Sea was a self-disclosure of God of which they could say, 'This is the Lord's doing and it is marvellous in our eyes'. In fact, the theology of the Old Testament is just such an interpretation of history.

But, though cradled in this Hebrew view of history, the Christian church gradually lost it, and from the Renascence onwards Greek views of history prevailed. Then, in the nineteenth century, the 'positivist' historians took over, causing that 'flight from history' among our theologians which we have mentioned. Now all is changed. Modern secular historians no longer believe there are such things as bare facts or events. There are only interpreted facts and events. Moreover, personal involvement in the historical challenges of his own time can bring the historian real understanding of the past. Therefore (to apply these new insights to our particular problem) the fact that the evangelists were Christian believers and wrote in the light of the resurrection helped rather than hindered them in the task to which they set their hand.

Such is Richardson's view, and he turns it at once on Bultmann and the extreme form critics. Discovering that the gospels were written from the viewpoint of the Easter faith, they wrongly concluded that they must be worthless as history. The faith of the church, says Richardson, is the channel through which the historical facts about Jesus were conveyed, and there is no other. And with this he boldly applies his principles to that event which for so many critics has been the very nub of the problem, the resurrection. The church did not create belief in Christ's resurrection; it was belief in the resurrection which created the church. And this alone, on purely critical grounds, provides a rational historical explanation of the available evidence. Therefore—

> We need not feel disconcerted ... by the discovery that all the Gospel records are written from the point of view of the Easter faith: historians always view events in the perspective of later developments, and the fact that the whole Gospel tradition bears testimony to Christ's resurrection is itself evidence, not that the Gospels are unhistorical, but that the resurrection is an event in history.

To which he adds (clearly with Bultmann in mind):

> There is no historical testimony at all to a non-kerygmatic Christ, a rabbi who summoned men to existential decision, and did not rise from the dead. And there is no reason to suppose that the Romans would have found it necessary to execute such a preacher, had he existed.[1]

III

Mention of Christ's resurrection leads on naturally to Wolfhart Pannenberg of Munich in whose 'theology of hope' that event is the diamond pivot on which all turns.

As preface to his views on history, let us summarize his doctrine of Christ's person as we find it in his *magnum opus, Jesus God and Man* (ET SCM Press and Westminster 1968. The 1964 German title was *Grundzüge der Christologie.*).

In his account of the God-man Pannenberg prefers the Christology which begins 'from below' and not 'from above'. In other words he starts not from the divine Logos but from the human Jesus, and thus avoids any suggestion of a God-man hybrid walking on the earth. For him, the paramount event in Jesus' story is his resurrection. This act of God once for all marked him out as the divine Son of God. No

subjective vision, or existential experience, the resurrection
is a real event in history and vital for Christian faith; for,
in the context of apocalyptic thought, it means that the end
of the world has begun. (Apocalyptic thought, be it noted,
is not merely something Jewish: it belongs to something
universally human – that 'open-ness' which hopes beyond
the existing world.)

It is (he begins) characteristic of man, as distinct from the
other animals, to think he was not made to die. Even when
faced with death, according to the medical psychologists, he
reaches out in thought to a future beyond it, believing that
in his earthly existence his true life is never fulfilled. This
is what underlay the apocalyptic belief that when we sleep
the sleep of death it is but to awake at God's touch to find
our true fulfilment.

Then he turns to the resurrection of Jesus. The earliest
Easter traditions are of two sorts: (1) testimonies to appear-
ances of the risen Lord (as in I Cor. 15), and (2) testimonies
to the empty tomb (as in Mark 16). Since these two strands
of tradition arose independently, they complement each other
and argue the facticity of the resurrection.

This is not just a historical event, but an eschatological
one. It is a divine fore-taste of the End-time, the God-given
pledge of general resurrection for his people. Explaining
late Judaism's doctrine of the resurrection of the body, which
he finds compatible with modern views of the body-soul
relation, he argues the hope of life beyond death for those
who are in Christ.

How then does Pannenberg unite God and man in Christ?
In the man Jesus we have the divine Son of God, not so
much because he spoke of his unity with the heavenly Father
but because, living in unbroken fellowship with him and
perfectly obeying that Father even in the agony of death,
he perfectly revealed God. On that life God set his seal by
raising him from the dead. Because of his perfect relationship with the Father, Jesus was the divine Son of God – for
only God can reveal God – and the event of the first Easter
Day vindicated that life and all that Jesus had claimed to be.

Here is the basis for the Christian hope. Since Jesus is
risen from the dead, the End-time has already broken into
history. His resurrection is at once pledge and pre-view of
future history and of man's final destiny in Christ.

IV

Here however our prime concern is with Pannenberg's view of revelatory history. Like Richardson, he founds on the Hebrew approach. Alone among the nations Israel saw history neither as the caprice of the gods nor as part of nature but as the workshop of the living God, the God who is 'compresent' to all times (past, present and future), the God who is for ever doing new things, but whose final purpose, pre-viewed in Christ's resurrection, will not be completely revealed until the End.

You cannot (he goes on, as Richardson had done) separate fact and significance. Facts are always experienced in a context in which they have meaning, and the interpretation is part of the event. Fact and interpretation form a unity, and the proper tool for its investigation is historical research.

How does an event mark itself out as revelatory? There are two criteria. One is its unpredictable novelty, its element of surprise – the very feature which historic Israel had often noted in God's dealings with them. The other is the recognition of the event as fulfilling hopes aroused by previous events, e.g., the Exodus and deliverance at the Red Sea.

But how can these two apparently incompatible things be combined so as to give unity to history? Only the concept of the living God, the creator of the ends of the earth and the Lord of history, enables us to grasp the unity of history so as to hold together the peculiar characteristics of the historical. (Here is a bold challenge to secular historians!)

Yet to this high concept of history a man may well demur, 'But surely the same event may hold different meanings for different people?' 'Agreed,' replies Pannenberg, 'but have you forgotten that critical historians have their own procedures for settling such differences of opinion? A historical conclusion may be regarded as morally certain when, having been exposed to all proper tests, it is found to correspond with the known facts. You *can* arrive at probable historical judgments.'

But if the objector is ready to agree thus far, he may now riposte: 'How can faith, which is total trust, found on such probable conclusions?' 'Why not,' returns Pannenberg, 'merely probable knowledge is perfectly compatible with faith of that kind.' Thus, to take a modern analogy, a man, after reading the Kinsey Report, may be aware that it is statistically probable that his wife is being unfaithful. This knowledge is nonetheless both psychologically and logically compatible with a trusting belief that she is in fact faithful.[2] But if history is the medium of divine revelation, revelation is not 'theophany' – that *direct* disclosure of the deity which is a common feature in pagan religions. Like what we call 'a broad hint', true revelation is ever *indirect*. (This is a welcome relief from that dubious supernaturalism which thinks of God as manifesting himself in isolated acts without the world's workaday happenings.) In human relations like friendship self-disclosure is mostly indirect. We know a man is our friend not because he expressly tells us so, but from his almost unconscious behaviour towards us. And thus did God reveal himself to Israel in events belonging to the workaday course of history.

In order to understand this indirect self-disclosure of God which culminates in Christ (John 1.18; II Cor. 4.6; Heb. 1.1f.), we need however more than just blind faith. As a basis for faith we require some reliable knowledge. And such trustworthy knowledge of Jesus – his self-understanding and his teaching – we have (*pace* Bultmann) in the gospel records.[3]

Christian faith then is not a leap in the dark. Rather is it a way of facing life, and especially the future, on the basis of lessons learned from revealing events in history, above all, the story of Israel which culminated in the coming of Christ, his resurrection and the rise of the new Israel, the church.

Pannenberg never pretends to have spoken the last word on theology. For him, it is always *in via*, since on his view the final truth about God will not be disclosed until the End-time. But his theology of hope is a fine cordial for drooping Christian spirits, as it recalls us to the centrality of the resurrection of Jesus for Christian faith.

What Richardson and Pannenberg between them have done is to take theology out of the ghetto into which it seemed to be relapsing. They have rightly insisted that the history with which the Christian theologian has to deal is actual history, and not some phoney 'supra history', and that the only way of settling historical questions is to employ the best methods of historical research. By doing so they have done much to restore historical study to its place of honour in what was once called 'the queen of the sciences' – theology.

NOTES

1. Richardson, op. cit., pp. 239f.
2. A. D. Galloway, *Wolfhart Pannenberg*, Allen & Unwin 1973, p. 48.
3. This solution to the problem of faith and knowledge goes back to Luther's distinction between *notitia* on the one hand and *fiducia* on the other.

3

Progress in
New Testament Theology

The man in the street, if he thinks of theology at all, tends to think of it as a static science. The physical and medical sciences are constantly advancing and making new discoveries. But she who was once called 'the queen of the sciences' does not. While they push ahead and make new conquests in the unknown, she remains not unlike –

> the Lady of the Mere
> Sole-sitting by the shores of old romance

content to hug fast her ancient treasures – 'the faith once for all delivered to the saints' – and unconcerned to understand it better or to apply it to the world of the twentieth century.

The man in the street is not wholly mistaken. The church is notoriously conservative and slow to adapt its message to a rapidly changing world. But, by the same token, the man in the street, shows himself unaware of the real advances that are being made in theology and of the pioneers and trail-blazers who are continually emerging. Harnack is succeeded by Barth, Barth by Tillich, Tillich by Bultmann, Bultmann by Pannenberg, and so on.

The purpose of this essay is to set down some of the real advances that have been made in New Testament theology, as I have seen them in my life-time.

I

If we could recall some scholar who had died at the turn of the century and show him some of the books now being written about the New Testament, the thing which would make him rub his eyes would not be our opinions on this or that critical or historical problem, but the whole tone and temper of our approach to New Testament theology. He could not fail to detect in our writing certain dominant notes little heard in 1900 – much talk about 'revelation', the rehabilitation of the word 'eschatology', a revived interest in the Old Testament as Christian scripture, a deep concern to stress the unity of the Bible and to see it as the record of the long unfolding of God's saving purpose, culminating in a great historic *crescendo*, the dawning of God's kingdom in the person and work of Christ.

Were our scholar to ask how and when this change had come about, we should have to tell him something of the tragic history of this twentieth century and of the theological awakening it had produced. The incendiary bomb which in 1940 set ablaze the London Natural History Museum might here serve us as a parable. Two months later, when the *débris* was cleared away, it was found that some rare and exotic seeds, a century and a half old, had begun to germinate under the influence of fire and hose-water. The ravages of war had awakened life in what had so long lain dormant. Even so, under the strains and stresses of two World Wars which rocked our civilisation to its foundations, the Bible and theology came alive again.

For our starting point we might take the year 1918 when Karl Barth threw his theological bomb – his extraordinary commentary on Romans – into the camp of the theologians. Its explosion had wide repercussions. Men began to take the Bible's way of looking at things with a new seriousness; and our theologians, so long preoccupied with Higher Criticism, comparative religion and psychology, were driven to consider whether after all this deserved the name of theology and whether, as Barth affirmed, there might not be an authentic word of God for the twentieth century in a letter written in a Corinthian back-street nineteen hundred years ago.

Of course 1918 was simply the climactic year for something which had been brewing for years. Long before the seeds of theological revival were being sown: sown in the decay of Liberalism and in the whole complex of world-events which culminated in the First World War. But it needed that catastrophe to convince most people of what strange and

terrible elements the world was made, how dread a labora-
tory of good and evil is the heart of man, and how inadequate
was the creed of Liberal Protestantism to provide the modern
Christian with a faith to live by in the day of the ordeal.[1]

Thus began what we call the revival in biblical theology,
bringing with it a flood of new books on the New Testament –
commentaries not content to be merely critical, theological
Word Books (of which the greatest was Kittel's), monographs
on this or that New Testament theme, (e.g., early Christian
worship) new books on the parables of Jesus (Dodd and
Jeremias), on eschatology and ethics (e.g., Amos Wilder),
on the Christian conception of time (Cullmann and Marsh),
on the person of Christ (e.g., those by Vincent Taylor and
Oscar Cullmann), and so on – all reflecting in one way or
another the 'new look' that had come over the New Testament. And so, inevitably, there began to appear new
theologies of the New Testament – by Stauffer, by Bultmann,
by Richardson, by Schnackenburger....

One point, however, should be underlined. The leaders
in this revival of biblical theology did not jettison the great
gains made by historical criticism in the hey-day of Liberalism, and retreat into 'fundamentalism'. Not less sure of the
necessity for criticism (which helps to disengage the kernel
from the husk, to save time often lost in the defence of outposts, and to clear the ground for the erection of a house of
doctrine on firm foundations), they were convinced that the
Bible is more than the record of man's religious development
from primitive beginnings, that we do not see it aright unless
we also see it as the only record of the redeeming love of God,
able to speak the word of salvation in Christ to us men in the
twentieth century.

II

What were the main trends in this revival? Perhaps the
best way to begin our reply is to ask two important questions
and then observe what answers were given them, first in 1900
and then nearly sixty years later:

(1) Is Christ part of the gospel which he preached?
(2) Is the church part of it also?

If you turn up Harnack's famous book *What is Christianity*
(1900), you will find that both questions are answered in the

negative. Christ did not conceive of himself as part of the good news he proclaimed, and the idea of the church had no place in his message. Now turn up *Christ and his Church* (1957) by Nygren (of *Agapē and Erōs* (1932-38) fame), and note what he says. First, the gospel is nothing other than a message about Christ (who embodies the kingdom of God); and second, the church is part of the gospel and 'a Christology that does not include an ecclesiology is false'[2].

Could there be a more complete *volte face* by scholarship? This example pinpoints two of the major trends which have marked the revival in Biblical theology, and which we may now discuss.

It is right that we should begin with *Christ* in whom all centres. First, then, we have returned to worthier ways of thinking about Jesus Christ. There has been a return to Christology, and it is in large measure due to the new insight into eschatology which we owe to Johannes Weiss and Albert Schweitzer. Liberalism gave us Jesus the religious genius. But the picture they drew of him was simply the idealized self-portrait of man in the nineteenth century – a lay figure not nearly big enough to explain the rest of the New Testament, let alone nineteen centuries of Christian experience. 'Why any man should have troubled to crucify the Christ of Liberal Protestantism,' wrote William Temple,[3] 'has always been a mystery.' That picture Schweitzer smashed beyond repair. If he himself remained to the end a Liberal, he provided the key for a new and better interpretation of the central figure in the New Testament. His claim on our gratitude is not only his wonderful later work as a Christian doctor in the swamps of Lambarene, but his insistence in *The Quest of the Historical Jesus* (A. & C. Black. 3rd ed. 1954) that *eschatology* is of primary importance for understanding his mission and message. What this means was well put years ago by F. R. Barry:[4]

> The whole story moves in an atmosphere of wonder, fringed, as it were, with a numinous corona whose flames leap up in immeasurable splendour into spaces which we cannot chart. We cannot tear it out of that setting. Apart from it there is no story to tell. And it is the triumph of the eschatologists to have recovered that atmosphere.

Of course Schweitzer did not use his new-found key aright,

and nowadays it is not hard to expose his capital errors –
his uncritical reliance on Matthew's gospel (and especially
Matt. 10.23) his blindness to those many sayings and parables
of Jesus which show that he thought of the kingdom of God
as an inbreaking reality in his ministry, and so on. But his
key was the right one, and his successors, using it to better
advantage, have given us a quite new conception of Christ
and the kingdom of God. For if the kingdom means not
some kind of earthly Utopia to be built by men on Christian
principles but the saving sovereignty of God breaking
decisively into human history for us men and our salvation,
and if Jesus is, as the gospels testify, the person in whose
ministry, death and resurrection that sovereignty is incarnated
in action, a very high Christology is plainly implied. We are
shown one conscious of being called to play a quite unique
part in the story of God's dealings with men. If the *Mysterium
Christi* remains, we now realize that we cannot tell the
Story of Jesus aright without talking christologically, and
the figure whom the eschatological reading of the gospels
reveals is one not unworthy to bear the weight of the tremendous claims made for him by St Paul, St Peter, St John, the
writer to the Hebrews and John the Seer who gave us the
Apocalypse.

The second trend, closely linked with the first, has been a
return to a worthier conception of *the church* and its place in
the New Testament scheme of things.

In the nineteenth century Liberal Protestantism refused
to take the idea of the church seriously. It was the age of
individualism. On the one hand, you had scholars confidently
declaring that Jesus never meant to create a new society.
Even as late as 1920, Lake and Jackson[5] could assure their
readers that 'Jesus in the earliest tradition does not appear
as intending to found a new society'. On the other hand, you
had ordinary Christians, calling themselves evangelicals, who
could be heard saying, 'Give us more Christianity and less
churchianity'. Small wonder the notion got about that the
church had no real place in essential Christianity.

Now, if there is one thing we are sure of, it is that the
church is basic to New Testament Christianity. Study a book
like R. N. Flew's *Jesus and his Church* (and a dozen more
like it could be named), and you begin to see that everything
in Jesus' preaching and teaching – his gospel of God's re-

deeming rule in action, his conception of his Messiahship, his words about the shepherd and his flock – demand, in spiritual logic, the creation of a new Israel, a new people of God, a church. The Messianic people cannot exist without the Messiah; the Messiah cannot be the Messiah without such a people. It has rightly been said that 'the discovery of the church's role in early Christianity is the greatest event in exegetical science in our generation'. Our scholars have now decided not only that Jesus intended an *ecclēsia*, but that the church is an integral part of God's saving activity in Christ.

A third feature, or trend, has been the re-discovery of the *essential unity* of the New Testament.

Liberal scholarship took the New Testament apart, analysing it into its various sources and strata. For this analytical work we must be grateful, but it inevitably produced a fragmentation of early Christian thought. It produced 'gospel scholars' 'Paulinists', Johannine experts etc., excellent men all, but men ever in peril of not seeing the wood for the particular theological trees which absorbed their special study. They forgot that 'it needs the whole of the New Testament to show who Christ is'. Sooner or later a change was bound to come.

Away back in 1905 P. T. Forsyth[6] had presciently written: 'The critical study of the Scriptures is at its best and Higher Criticism at its highest, when it passes from being analytic and becomes synthetic. And the synthetic principle is the Gospel.' But he was a voice crying in the Liberal wilderness. Thirty years later, the greatest British New Testament scholar of our time, C. H. Dodd, in his inaugural lecture at Cambridge, affirmed 'the present task in New Testament studies' to be one of synthesis, and in book after splendid book illustrated what he meant. In the years that followed most of us followed his lead.

The older approach to the New Testament had stressed the varieties of New Testament thought; the newer approach discloses basic unity underlying diversity. We now see that the gospel of the kingdom of God (the theme of the Synoptic Gospels) is the Word of life (St John) which is in turn the gospel of Christ (St Paul), and that to be 'in the kingdom of God' means to 'have eternal life' and to be 'in Christ' (who *is* the kingdom of God and the bearer of eternal life). Through all the undoubted diversities of the New Testament, we can trace a common message of salvation (the *kērygma*), a common doctrine of the divine society which it created, and a common attitude of faith to him who was the central figure in the divine drama of our redemption.

III

Now let us consider some by-products of this renascence in biblical theology, starting with the 'demythologizing' controversy.

Between the two World Wars our scholars (notably C. H. Dodd) rediscovered the *kērygma*, or earliest apostolic gospel, and we all began again to preach 'the mighty acts of God' of which the New Testament is the record. But is it enough to proclaim the apostolic gospel today when it clearly comes to us embedded in the images of first-century mythology? How can modern man accustomed to use electric light and to think in scientific ways, accept such outmoded thought-forms?

This was the question Rudolph Bultmann posed in the early nineteen-forties when 'the cold war' was just beginning to 'hot up'. What were the 'myths' he had in mind? The Bible's three-decker concept of the world, was one of course. But Bultmann went a good deal further; by 'myths' he meant also the belief in demons, miracles, the pre-existence of Christ, the doctrine of his death as a sacrifice, and even the resurrection as a historical fact.

Shall we then dismiss the gospel as a bunch of exploded myths? No, said Bultmann, myths are the deepest clue to history because they are the ancient way of describing human existence, and the gospel can still be made relevant to modern man if we will take the trouble to re-interpret them in terms of Martin Heidegger's existentialist philosophy of 'Being'. Here is a cradle in which it can be laid without adulterating its essential message and with the hope of making it speak to man's condition today.

So began a debate, of which the end is not yet, though it is nearing stalemate. As it progressed, men began to realize that Bultmann's proposal to translate the myths entirely into non-mythical language could not be carried through without draining most of the life-blood from the Christian faith.

This was the point of T. W. Manson's *mot*: 'Bultmann proposes to give us Christianity without tears. What he gives us is tears without Christianity.' Moreover, when Christian philosophers like David Cairns examined the Heideggerian new 'cradle' for the gospel, their fear grew that, so far from being a safe nest for the gospel, it might well turn out to be a cuckoo which, unless faithfully dealt with, would shoulder the Christian fledglings from the nest!

Some demythologizing of the gospel every Christian preacher worthy of his salt must do if he is to communicate effectively to modern man. But this is another matter from assenting to Bultmann's radical remedies. To endorse them in their entirety is to run the risk of preaching 'another gospel' – a gospel of self-salvation in which Jesus becomes simply the opportunity for man to save himself by making the right decision. On the contrary, we must insist that the Christian religion, when it seeks to express the transcendent and ineffable, must resort to 'myth' – that is, the expression in story form of theological truth that cannot readily be communicated in any other way. For 'myth' can be, and often is,

> ... the language which contains the clue
> To that which is at once both real and true.

A second by-product was the valuable debate (to be discussed in a later essay) set agoing by Karl Barth in 1943 when, shocked by the pagan behaviour of the 'German Christians', he took up cudgels on behalf of believers' baptism and provoked a powerful riposte from Oscar Cullmann and Joachim Jeremias in defence of infant baptism.

And a third was 'the new look' that, from the nineteen-forties onwards, came over the Fourth Gospel.

A generation ago Kirsopp Lake could write, 'John (i.e., the gospel) may contain a few fragments of true tradition, but in the main it is fiction'. In 1963 C. H. Dodd showed that 'behind the Fourth Gospel lies an ancient tradition independent of the other Gospels and meriting serious consideration as a contribution to our knowledge of the historical facts concerning Jesus Christ'.

New and older manuscripts of the gospel have come to light. The Dead Sea Scrolls have shown its basic background to be Palestinian. The spade of the archaeologist has, at this point and that, vindicated the accuracy of its topography.

Above all, there has been a growing consensus of opinion that St John, so far from depending on the Synoptic Gospels, had access to old and independent tradition about Jesus, which may well go back to the apostle John. In short, the days are long past when we could say, If the Fourth Gospel contradicts the Synoptics, so much the worse for the Fourth Gospel. Not only does St John bring out the ultimate meaning of the gospel –

> Word of the Father
> Now in flesh appearing –

but at the beginning, the middle and the end he sheds light – historical light – on the story of Jesus, which we cannot neglect.

IV

Such is the present state of New Testament theology as one man sees it. Yet every revival like this runs the risk that when 'the first fine glorious rapture' has faded, it may degenerate into some sort of scholasticism (as the rich insights of the Reformation ran out into the arid divinity of the seventeenth century). What has been a healthy stream watering the life of the church may become a stagnation of knowledge which, because of its obscurity, cannot become incarnate in Christian life. When Donald Mackinnon writes of 'the pseudo-biblicism which frequently does duty for theology today,' he has clearly this danger in mind. There is a theology which is little more than a product of Greek grammar or Hebrew syntax or which bandies about polysyllabic wonders like 'kerygmatic' or 'eschatological' and darkens counsel with ill-defined words. Yet all sound Christian theology should be, in some sense, what Matthew Arnold called literature, 'a criticism of life' – the life of man in relation to the will of God revealed in Christ. Only if we keep our biblical theology in healthy contact with the life not merely of the church but of the wider world, shall we save it from scholasticism.

What will be the value of all our new insights into New Testament theology[7] if they cannot be imparted to the rank and file of our fellow-Christians in terms which will come home to their business and bosoms?

Take one example. The discovery by our scholars of the true meaning of the kingdom of God in the gospels seems to me the most important achievement made by our modern biblical theologians. God's kingdom is *not* some sort of Super Welfare State under Christian auspices or some kind of earthly paradise to be set up by men. It means the kingly rule or reign of God, and it is nothing if it is not divine and dynamic. It is a 'break-through' from the unseen world – God in his royal power, and in fulfilment of his promises, invading human history to rescue his people from their sins and woes. More, it is the very heart of the New Testament's good news that God's reign really and decisively began when he sent his messianic Son by his ministry, death and resurrection, to reconcile a sinful world to himself.

This new understanding of this key New Testament phrase is still however the *peculium* of specialists. It has not yet reached the man in the pew who, when he hears the phrase, still thinks of man striving and not of God acting, and acting once for all. (Not that the petition in the Lord's Prayer is a call to human quiescence!) Yet unless this new insight can be embodied in the preaching, life and thought of the church, will it be any more than a passing phase in theology?

The conclusion is plain. We biblical scholars have not done our work until our new insights in theology have been so simplified and 'communicated' that they will come home with vital interest and power to the man or the woman in the congregation or the lad and the lass in the Bible class.

There is only one way in which this can be done – by a much closer cooperation between those who theologize and those who preach and teach. 'If kings were philosophers or philosophers kings,' said James Denney,[8] 'we should have the ideal state according to Plato. If evangelists were our theologians, or theologians our evangelists, we should at least be nearer the ideal Church.'

NOTES

1. On the failure of Liberalism to interpret the Bible as the Word of God see T. W. Manson's brilliant essay in *The Interpretation of the Bible*, ed. C. W. Dugmore, 1944.

2. A. Nygren, *Christ and His Church*, SPCK 1957, p. 31.

3. *Readings in St John's Gospel*, 1942, Macmillan 1974 ed., p. xxvii.

4. *The Relevance of Christianity*, 1931, p. 98.

5. F. J. Foakes-Jackson and Kirsopp Lake (eds), *The Beginnings of Christianity*, 1920, vol. I, p. 317.

6. *The Contemporary Review*, October 1905, p. 579.

7. I have summarized the 'new look' in my *According to John*, SCM Press 1968. But *the* book on the subject is C. H. Dodd's *Historical Tradition in the Fourth Gospel*, Cambridge University Press 1963.

8. *The Death of Christ*, Tyndale 1951, p. viii.

4

Grammar and Godliness

The story is told of 'Rabbi' Duncan, the celebrated professor in New College, Edinburgh, that he once said to some young men going out into the church's ministry, 'What you need are the three G's – Greek, Grace and Gumption. If you haven't Greek, you can learn it. If you haven't Grace, you can pray for it. But if you haven't Gumption, the Lord help you!'

Today the first 'G' in the triad is ceasing to be a *desideratum*. Gone are the days when a Dr Johnson could say, 'Sir, Greek is like old lace, every man gets as much of it as he can'. In our science-dominated schools Greek is on the way out, and in Scotland you may now gain a baccalaureate in divinity without even a smattering of it.

Yet, despite our wealth of good modern translations of the New Testament, a knowledge of Greek will undoubtedly make a man a better interpreter of gospel and epistle, as it will help him to decide which modern rendering best reproduces the original meaning of evangelist and apostle. We may smile at Browning's Grammarian who –

> settled *Hoti's* business – let it be! –
> Properly based *Oun*,
> Gave us the doctrine of the enclitic *De* –[1]

but the man who can read 'the words which the Holy Spirit teaches' (I Cor. 2.13) in the original tongue will, other things being equal, be a better herald of the gospel than his Greekless brother. Godliness can be enriched by grammar.

I

Bishop B. F. Westcott was one of the three great New

Testament scholars Cambridge produced last century – the others being F. J. A. Hort and J. B. Lightfoot. Oral tradition has it that one day he was accosted by a Salvation Army lass with, 'Sir, are you saved?' The Bishop is said to have replied, 'Do you mean *sōtheis*, or *sesōsmenos*, or *sōzomenos*?' These are three Greek participles of the verb to 'save' – one an aorist, the second a perfect, and the third a present. And the point of Westcott's answer is that the English word 'saved' lacks the precision of the Greek, and is patient of three different shades of meaning – 'saved', 'having been saved' and 'being saved'.

Let this story introduce a brief study of the exegetical and theological value of a knowledge of Greek. In what is a vast field let us single out two matters – Greek prepositions and Greek verb tenses.

II

For those who have eyes to see them there are pictures in Greek prepositions. Take *anti* for example. Originally meaning 'opposite', it came to mean 'in front of' (as in Heb. 12.2 'the joy set *before* him) and finally 'in place of' as in the great 'ransom' saying (Mark 10.45). Noteworthy is St John's *charin anti charitos* 'grace for grace', suggesting wave upon wave of grace. Conjoin *anti* with *syn* 'together with' and put them before a verb like *lambanesthai* 'take hold of', as is done in Luke 10.40, and Martha's word to Jesus, about Mary becomes more vivid. 'Bid her,' she says to Jesus 'take hold along with me' (*synantilabētai*). The picture is of the two sisters, opposite each other, doing the work jointly.

But prepositions can involve high doctrine like that of Christ's *kenōsis* (literally 'emptying') as expounded by theologians like P. T. Forsyth and H. R. Mackintosh. Critics of the doctrine like William Temple may ask, 'What was happening to the rest of the universe during the time that the Creative Word was so self-emptied as to have no being except in the infant Jesus?' The implication is that a kenotic Christology entails cosmic chaos. But nowhere does the New Testament teach that the universe was created by the Son. In such 'creative' contexts the preposition employed is not *hypo* 'by' but generally *dia* 'through', and sometimes *en* 'in'. This is true of Paul, of John and of Hebrews. 'The New

Testament,' says Vincent Taylor, 'holds fast to the belief that God is the Creator and speaks of the Logos or the Son as the agent or medium of creation.'[2]

En is the Greek for 'in'. Because it is so freely and widely used in the New Testament, J. H. Moulton (who was anything but a dry-as-dust grammarian) called it the prepositional 'maid of all work'. But from its use in the famous phrase *en Christō*, 'in Christ' it might equally be called 'the handmaid of the Lord'. (If we count by-forms of it like 'in the Lord' and 'in Him', it occurs some two hundred times in the New Testament.) What is the force of *en* in it? Once it was said to carry a 'mystical' sense. If by 'mystical' is meant union with the living Christ, no objection need be taken. Yet in the light of recent study of the phrase, it might well be named 'corporate', since Christ in the phrase is a 'societary' person – a person implying a community. In passage after New Testament passage to be 'in Christ' is to be a member of the community of which he is the living head. This is why the New English Bible again and again translates 'incorporate in Christ' (e.g. Eph. 1.1; Col. 1.1; Phil. 1.1; 3.8). It is a salutary reminder that no man can be a Christian by himself, that all true Christian experience is ecclesiastical experience.

III

Remembering Westcott's hesitations about the word 'saved', let us turn now to Greek verbs and their tenses.

The first point to seize about Greek tenses – present, imperfect, 'aorist' (literally 'unbounded') and perfect – is that they express not so much the *time* as the *kind of action* involved. Someone has likened the action expressed by the aorist tense to the single exposure of a camera in a snap-shot, the imperfect (and often the present) to the continuous exposure of a motion picture camera, and the perfect to the initial exposure plus the subsequent development of the picture. In other words, the aorist describes *events*, the imperfect (and the present) *proceedings*, and the perfect *results*.

The two versions of the Lord's Prayer, in the 'bread' petition, exemplify the difference between the aorist which denotes 'punctiliar' action (action regarded as a point), and the present whose force is 'linear,' i.e., durative. In Matthew we have 'Give (*dos*: aorist imperative) us this day our daily bread' (Matt. 6.11): in Luke, 'Keep on giving (*didou*, present imperative) us each day our daily bread' (Luke 11.3).

The force of the imperfect may be illustrated from Mark's story of the Strange Exorcist (Mark 9.38-41). When the disciples told Jesus that they had forbidden the exorcist to expel demons in his name because 'he was not one of us', Jesus rebuked them. 'We tried to prevent him' (*ekōluomen*: imperfect tense), they explained. Jesus replied *Mē kōluete* (present tense) – 'stop trying to prevent him, for he who is not against us is on our side'.

Perhaps the best example of the theological value of Greek grammar is provided by the use of the aorist *edōken* 'gave' in John 3.16 (called by Luther 'the Gospel within the Gospels'). St John might have written *hōste dounai* 'so as to give', to mark the measure of God's potential gift in Christ his Son. Instead, he writes *hōste edōken* 'so that he gave' (an aorist which includes the cross as well as the incarnation), to declare the magnitude of the recorded act.[3]

A final example, showing the force of the perfect tense in Greek, occurs in I Cor. 15.3ff. where Paul is citing the witnesses to the reality of Christ's resurrection. In the midst of nine verbs in the aorist tense Paul elects to employ the perfect tense (*egēgertai*) when he refers to Christ's resurrection. For him, this event had a different significance from Christ's death and burial, so that he deliberately switched from plain 'punctiliar' aorists to a pregnant perfect. For *egēgertai* means, 'He was raised and remains risen – still lives today.'[4] For, as he explained elsewhere (Rom. 6.9), 'Christ being raised from the dead will never die again; death no longer has dominion over him'.

Such are some of the finer shades of meaning which a knowledge of New Testament Greek will bring to the student. If it be replied that they mostly concern prepositional and verbal niceties, may we not rejoin with Renan that 'truth consists in the *nuances*'?

NOTES

1. 'A Grammarian's Funeral'.
2. *The Person of Christ*, Macmillan 1958, p. 267.
3. W. F. Howard, *Christianity according to St John*, 1943, p. 63.
4. Another good example in *kekathiken*, perfect of *kathizein*, in Heb. 12.2. It means 'has taken his seat and remains sitting'.

5

The Blessedness of Mary

Luke 1.26-38

One morning last century (probably not long after the **Papal Bull** about the Immaculate Conception) the noted Aberdeen divine, Dr Kidd of Gilcolmston, meeting the local priest, greeted him as follows: 'Hello, priest Fraser. Tell me this. What is the difference between Christ's mother and my mother?' 'I don't know, Doctor,' replied the priest, 'but there is a very great difference between the sons.' *'Touché!'* the Doctor might graciously have replied, but it is not recorded that he did.

Whether he was aware of it or not, priest Fraser was making a point that the polemical Protestant is in danger of forgetting – that Mary was the mother of one he acknowledges as the divine Son of God.

Rightly does the Protestant repudiate the excesses of Mariolatry. Rightly does he protest that Rome accords to 'Mary his mother' attributes and prerogatives which find no warrant in scripture and beggar modern man's belief. Loth to believe that the cult of the Holy Mother has exercised a civilizing influence on European life and thought (thought, as Sir Kenneth Clark has shown, it has), he denounces the worship of Mary as blasphemous, and – if he knows his scriptures – can find on Jesus' own lips a discouragement of the 'beatification' of Mary:

> A woman in the crowd raised her voice and said to him, 'Blessed is the womb that bore you and the breasts you sucked!' But he said, 'Blessed rather are those who hear the word of God and keep it!' (Luke 11.27f.).

Yet in his recoil from the errors of Rome the Protestant may do less than honour to 'Mary his mother', refusing her the reverence which is her due.

Luke's story of the annunciation tells how God sent the angel Gabriel 'with a message for a girl called Mary, betrothed to a man named Joseph', and how, while still a virgin, by the Holy Spirit's help, she conceived her first-born son. Here we are moving in the realm of religious 'myth' (which does not of course mean 'fairy story'). By means of his 'mythical' story Luke means us to understand (1) that in the birth of the Saviour God was specially at work, and (2) that it involved the physiological miracle of virginal conception. At this point the interminable argument about virgin birth usually breaks out, so that we miss another important element in the story.

Divinely told that she should bear a son to be called Jesus, Mary was also assured that he should be Israel's long-expected Davidic Messiah, bear the title 'Son of the Most High', and reign for ever. To her modest demurring, 'How can this be, since I know not a man?' came the reply that with God nothing is impossible. Whereupon she answered, 'Behold the handmaid of the Lord! Be it unto me according to thy word!' Mary's *Ecce ancilla Domini!* (how lovely is the Latinity of it) was the answer of her faith to the message of God's grace.

All this reminds us of Paul's argument about Abraham's faith in Rom. 4 (which, though it strikes us as rabbinic, rightly insists that faith did not begin with Christianity but lies at the heart of all true religion).

When Abraham and Sarah seemed too old to have a family, God promised them a son and a great posterity. It seemed a thing impossible which nonetheless befell. Against all the odds, Abraham took God at his word, and his faith, instead of wilting, grew ever stronger. This faith God counted to him for righteousness. God justified him for his faith. But if God justified Abraham for his faith, did not Mary similarly find acceptance with God for her faith and become the mother of the saviour? By the very doctrine that the Protestant holds dearest – justification by faith in response to God's grace – Mary was as right with God as mortal can be.

Now return to the point from which we started. If there is no scriptural warrant for the worship of Mary, is it not intelligible and even natural that men should have come to revere Mary as unique, saying in the words of the beautiful old ballad –

Mother and maiden,
　Was never none but she,
Well may such a maiden
　Goddes mother be.

Here some theologically-minded Protestant may object that it is what is implied by 'Mother and maiden' which he cannot credit. If there was to be a true incarnation, Jesus must have had normal human parentage. By rejecting the story of Jesus' birth without a human father he is apt to imagine that he has got rid of the whole idea of a miraculous birth. It is not so. If the Son of God was born as other men are, a miracle still remains. If the physiological miracle is repudiated, we are yet left with a metaphysical one – the coming of the divine Son of God into human life, born of a human mother.

(We once heard Paul Tillich describe the doctrine of the Virgin Birth as the first appearance of docetism in Christianity. Docetism is the heresy that Christ was a divine being who only *seemed* to be human – in fact he did not take our nature on him, or suffer and die. But is it not equally possible that the doctrine was an answer to that very emergent heresy, an insistence that the Son of God was born of a human mother?)

How shall we sum up? In spite of Luke 11.27f., a Protestant no less than a Roman Catholic ought to be able to pronounce a 'makarism' upon Mary, saying 'Blessed art thou among women'. If he may not worship her, she deserves his deepest reverence. Through Mary the eternal Son of God assumed a servant's form for us men and our salvation. And if Mary said, 'Behold the handmaid of the Lord! Be it unto me according to thy word!' she is as worthy in God's sight as mortal can be. For justification by faith is our only righteousness. None can say more than this, and none do better.

6

Christ's Baptism and Ours

Only the older among us will recall the 'German Christians'. They were Protestants who, during the Hitler *régime*, sought to accommodate Christianity to Nazism which was rabidly anti-semitic. Accordingly, they scrapped the Old Testament, pronounced the sense of sin a delusion of the synagogue, and dismissed Paul as 'the Rabbi'. So shocked by their paganizing of Christianity was Karl Barth that he wrote a little book[1] in which he boldly espoused believers' baptism. The church, he said, ought not to baptize any but those who were old enough to make sincerely the conscious response of Christian faith. From outside the ranks of the Baptists had arisen a theological Goliath to defend the most distinctive article in their Christian thinking. Naturally, they were much encouraged.

While the Second World War still raged, no measured reply to Barth was forthcoming. It came in 1948 when Barth found a foeman worthy of his steel in Oscar Cullmann whose book[2] set going among scholars a debate which was to shed long-lost light on Christian initiation as the New Testament understands it.

Inevitably much of the scholars' argument was above the heads of ordinary church people who continued to believe that baptism was the dedicating of their child to God or the rite at which 'the baby got its name'. Yet out of the debate came a 'new look' on the meaning of Christian baptism. Hitherto, for its dominical authority, many had depended on a doubtful text in Matt. 28.19.[3] Now they were given a whole network of proof that Baptism goes back not merely to the beginning of the Christian church but to the mind and purpose of Christ himself; for behind Christian baptism stands his own baptism, that general baptism for all men which began when he stepped down into Jordan and which he consummated on Calvary's hill.

If we are to understand the claim made in this last sentence, we shall have to go back to Christ's own baptism in Jordan by John, study its relation to his Passion which he called his 'baptism', and consider the church's 'coming of age' at Pentecost when, with the gift of the Holy Spirit, what we call Christian baptism began. In other words, we are concerned with three *kairoi*, times charged with divine moment and meaning, two in the earthly ministry of Jesus, and one in the initial rise of the New Israel which is Christ's Body, the church.

I

Before his mission to men began, there came for Jesus the first *kairos* which was to give its character to his whole ministry (Mark 1.4-9). Together with a crowd of sinful men, he went down into Jordan to be baptized by John. This baptism was 'for the forgiveness of sins'; but what sins had Jesus to confess? It was 'a baptism of repentance', but Jesus was repenting not for his own sins but for the sins of 'the many'. As he rose from the waters of Jordan, God's voice declared him his Son in words which described his sonhood in terms of Isaiah's Servant of the Lord (Isa. 42.1).

What was Jesus doing in having himself baptized? He was deliberately 'numbering himself with the transgressors' (Isa. 53.12). He was entering on his work as the Servant Messiah. What we call the atonement had begun. His baptism in Jordan was the beginning of that baptism of vicarious suffering for men's sins which was to be completed on the cross.

II

Turn now to the second *kairos*. Towards the end of his ministry, on the road to Jesusalem and in the *penumbra* of his Passion, came a like dramatic time which Jesus explicitly called his 'baptism'. When the sons of Zebedee requested Jesus for the chief places in his coming glory, Jesus spoke of the 'baptism' he was undergoing, and promised James and John that they would share in it. Clearly he was thinking of his passion and death, for only in the cross could his baptism become truly inclusive and vicarious (Mark 10.35-45).

Even more illuminating is that passage in Luke's gospel (probably derived from 'Q'), taut with all the tension of one 'already dwelling in his Passion', in which Jesus spoke of the climax of his ministry as a 'baptism':

> I have come to send fire on the earth, and how I wish it were already kindled! But I have a baptism to undergo, and how constricted I am until the ordeal is over! (Luke 12.49f.).

The words 'I have come to send fire on the earth' should be interpreted in the light of John the Baptist's prophecy about his great successor, 'He will baptize you with the Holy Spirit and with fire' (Luke 3.16; Matt. 3.11). Here is the link, not otherwise clear, between the 'fire' of v. 49 and the 'baptism' of v. 50. The purpose of Jesus' mission is to unloose in the world the pentecostal fire of the Spirit, which must, initially, be a fire of judgment. How Jesus wishes it were already kindled! 'But I have a baptism to undergo,' he says, clearly thinking of the cross. The outpouring of the Spirit awaits the completion of his baptism in death. St John took the point when he wrote: 'As yet the Spirit had not been given, because Jesus was not yet glorified' (John 7.39). So did the old commentator Bengel when he wrote of the first Whitsunday, 'On that day *the fire was lit*'.

But this is to anticipate the third *kairos* in which the potency of Christ's 'baptism' was to become available for all by the gift of the Holy Spirit. Meantime, let us turn from the gospels to the man who has been well named 'the fifth evangelist'. Writing to the Romans about AD 57, and appealing to what was a matter of common Christian belief, Paul says that we Christians are 'baptized into the *death* of Christ' (Rom. 6.3). What he means is that behind what we call Christian baptism stands Christ's general baptism, unique and all-inclusive, which he underwent for the sins of the world. As Cullmann puts it:

> According to the New Testament, all men have in principle received baptism long ago, namely on Golgotha, Good Friday and Easter. There the essential act of baptism was carried out, entirely without our cooperation, and even without our faith. There the world was baptized on the ground of the absolutely sovereign act of God who in Christ 'first loved us', even before we loved him, even before we believed.[4]

But is not Cullmann overplaying his hand when he says that this is the New Testament doctrine of baptism? On the contrary, it can be shown[5] that right through the New Testament documents – from Paul's letters and John's to Hebrews, I Peter and the Apocalypse – Christian baptism is connected with Christ's death. The work of Christ conceived as a single, prevenient and all-inclusive baptism for sinners is one of the major categories in the New Testament doctrine of salvation, and as we have seen, it derives from the mind and purpose of Jesus himself.

III

We turn now to the third *kairos* – the release of the Holy Spirit at Pentecost (Acts 2).

In Acts 1 Luke makes quite explicit the concept of the first Whitsunday miracle as a 'baptism'. 'You must wait in Jerusalem' the risen Lord tells his disciples, 'for the promise made by my Father ... John, as you know, baptized with water, but you will be baptized with the Holy Spirit, and within the next few days' (Acts 1.4f.).

And so they were when at Pentecost the infant church became the locus of the Holy Spirit. It is the third and last act in the drama of God's saving work in Christ. Hitherto the Spirit had been confined to the representative figure of Jesus, the Servant of the Lord (Luke 4.18ff.). Now it is outpoured on all, and from this event follows the new era of the church when the potency of Christ's baptism is made available for all who believe. Christian baptism – by water, in the name of Christ – is only possible after the church has become the place of the Spirit's indwelling. What happened collectively at Pentecost is henceforward to happen for each individual in the sacrament of the transmission of the Spirit. So on that day when men 'from every nation under heaven' experienced that 'uprush of new life' from the Spirit, 'the Lord and giver of life', Peter, the man on whom Jesus promised he would build his new people of God, said: 'Repent, and be baptized every one of you in the name of Jesus Christ for the forgiveness of your sins; and you shall receive the gift of the Holy Spirit. For the promise is to you and your children and to all that are far off, everyone whom the Lord our God calls to him' (Acts 2.38f.).

We latter-day Christians belong to those 'that are far off'. But though –

> The centuries go gliding,
> Yet still we have abiding
> With us that Spirit Holy,
> To make us brave and lowly[6] –

and when we are baptized, it is 'for the forgiveness of sins', that forgiveness which God wrought in Christ's baptism, and which first became effective for all at Pentecost. In union with Christ, our risen and regnant saviour, and by the work of the Holy Spirit, we are included in his vicarious repentance for sinners in Jordan, and we share in the redemption which he, as God's servant Son, accomplished for us at the cross and in its shining sequel. Named as his at our baptism, we are by that sacramental act set decisively within the Body of Christ. As members of his church, we become part of Him.

IV

So far, good – it is great gain to have had Christian baptism set back on to its original New Testament base, namely, the one great baptism of Christ for the world's sins. But, as a result, has not the case for infant baptism been gravely weakened? Those in the New Testament who underwent Christian baptism were normally adults who consciously had professed their Christian faith. Nowadays when infant baptism is the norm in most churches, the babies whom parents bring to the baptismal font can have little if any idea of what is happening to them. Indeed their sole contribution to the ceremony may well sound like a howl of protest at what is being done! Is infant baptism really compatible with New Testament doctrine and practice? We believe it is, and for three reasons.

The first is *historical*. When we read of whole 'households' being baptized (I Cor. 1.16; Acts 16.15, 33; 18.8), it is hard to believe that the children were not included. (At a Jewish proselyte's baptism, his children were baptized along with him.) To judge from Col. 2.11-13, it appears that about AD 60 Christian baptism was considered as the counterpart of Jewish circumcision (so Jeremias). It may well have been a controversy over the baptism of children which led to the inclusion in the gospel tradition of the story of Jesus blessing the children and telling the disciples not to 'forbid' (*kōluein*) them to come to him, for the Greek verb was firmly associated with baptism in the early church (Acts 8.36; 10.47; 11.17. Cf. Matt. 13.14).[7] In short, it is probable that the practice of infant baptism goes back to New Testament times.

The next argument is *theological*. Baptism *unto* faith (infant baptism) has as good a right in the principle of the gospel where *grace precedes faith*, as baptism *upon* faith (believers' baptism). The primacy of grace is well illustrated in Forsyth's parable of the christening mug.[8]

A child's grandmother sometimes presents him with a christening mug which he uses when he becomes big enough to sit at table with his elders. But the day comes when the child asks who gave him the mug. He is told that it was his grandmother who loved his as a little child. 'Where is she?' 'She is dead.' 'And she loved me as soon as I was born?' 'Yes.' So love comes home to the child as a beautiful thing, an unseen mysterious thing, a thing that was about his very beginning, and yet a thing that goes about him every day. The gift of the mug is Christian baptism. It is a sign and seal of the prevenient grace of God, of the love which went to the cross for our redeeming.

Finely did Bernard Manning say, 'Every time we baptize a child we declare to the world that what God does for us, he does without our merits, and even without our know-ledge.'[9] To the primacy and prevenience of that divine grace infant baptism offers vivid and unmistakable witness. It cannot then be unchristian to commit a child in baptism and cast the mantle of God's grace over him in his infancy, provided we insist that the process of Christian initiation will not be complete until the child, grown to years of discretion, confirms for himself the vows once taken on his behalf and, by conscious profession of his faith, is admitted to the full communion of the church.

The third argument, which is *corporate and vicarious*, is wholly in line with biblical religion (which has no place for a false individualism, for it 'knows nothing of solitary religion'), and can appeal to the mind of Christ himself. It is the principle that the faith of one or more persons can avail for another. You will find it illustrated in Mark's story of the Epileptic Boy (Mark 9.14-29) where Christ accepts the father's faith on behalf of the helpless lad. You will find it even more clearly in Mark's earlier story about the paralytic who was brought by his four friends to Jesus (Mark 2.1-12). 'When Jesus saw *their* faith,' we read, 'he said to the paralysed man, "My son, your sins are forgiven" '. The beginning of that man's new life was due not to his own act but to something his friends did for him, in respect not only of healing but of the forgiveness of sins.

Do not these two gospel stories have a bearing on infant baptism? Thanks to those who took us to the font in our infancy, many of us became members of Christ's church *in petto* (in reserve) before we ever could be aware of it. All unbeknown to us, through the faith of others, came the gift of God's grace in Christ. Does not infant baptism gather up this truth into one significant and moving symbol?

NOTES

1. *The Church's Teaching about Baptism*, ET 1948.
2. *Baptism in the New Testament*, SCM Press 1950.
3. There is evidence that 'baptizing them in the name of the Father, the Son and the Holy Spirit' does not go back to the dawn of Christianity when baptism was 'in the name of Christ'.
4. Cullmann, op. cit., p. 23.
5. See J. A. T. Robinson, *Twelve New Testament Studies*, SCM Press 1962, pp. 158-175.
6. F. C. Burkitt.
7. Cullmann, op. cit., pp. 71ff.
8. P. T. Forsyth, *Church and Sacraments*, 1916, p. 162.
9. *Why not Abandon the Church?*, 1939, p. 48.

7

The Egoism of Christ

How should a modern Christian think about the king and head of the church? If he is 'honest to God', says John Robinson, he will think of him as 'the Man for others'. Altruism means living and acting for others. Dr Robinson is therefore inviting us to see in Jesus God's altruism incarnate. This, he says, is what the New Testament writers mean when they say 'God was in Christ' or 'What God was, the Word was'. Because Jesus was utterly and completely 'the man for others', because he was love, he was 'one with the Father', because 'God is love'.

We doubt very much whether Paul or John would have approved this version of their thinking about Christ. But true it is that the Jesus of the gospels, from Jordan to Calvary, lived, suffered and died for others because he knew himself so commissioned to do by his heavenly Father.

I

Yet if Jesus was the great altruist, he was just as truly the great egoist. 'Egoism', from the personal pronoun *ego* (Greek and Latin) means for us self-regardingness, self-centredness, selfishness. It is not a lovely trait of character. We dislike the man through whose whole speech pulsates that horrid little pronoun 'I', and we would fain deal with him as Carlyle once did with an opinionative young egoist who talked about himself for a whole evening in Carlyle's house. As the Sage of Chelsea saw him out at the door, he said grimly, 'Empty yourself now, young man, for this is the last time you will ever cross my threshold'.

In that pejorative sense of the word our Lord certainly was no egoist. And yet how frequently, how magisterially, how royally the first personal pronoun occurs on the lips of 'the man for others'!

Some sixty times, according to the Synoptic Gospels, Jesus prefaced a momentous saying with an 'Amen I tell you'. 'Amen' is a Hebrew word of assent meaning 'truly' which the Christians took over from the Jews and used to signify audible agreement at the end of prayer, scripture-reading or hymn. By contrast, Jesus often began a saying with an 'Amen' followed by an 'I tell you'. To this *façon de parler*, this idiosyncrasy of speech, Jewish literature provides no parallel. It is what our learned men call an *ipsissima vox* – a unique feature – of Jesus' speaking-style. Nowadays, when a man says, 'I'm telling you', most of us resent the implied tone of superiority. Yet arrogance of this kind there was none in Christ's 'Amen I tell you'. For when we study his 'Amen' sayings in their contexts, we find that he regards his utterances as not his own but God's. He is speaking as his Father has bidden him (John 12.49); he is passing on what he has himself received from on high. This is not egoism in our sense of the word; it is obedience, obedience by Jesus to that living and holy Father who was for him the last reality in the world.

But this is only a beginning. Consider, next, the 'I-sayings' of Jesus – those sentences in which the emphatic pronoun *ego* dominates the speech. (If you do not read Greek, you may well miss this 'egoism'. The form of the Greek verb includes not only the action but the person doing it. Thus *lego* means 'I say', and it is unnecessary to put *ego* before it because the ending *o* indicates the person speaking. Only when special emphasis is required does Greek insert the *ego*. In English the best way of representing this is to italicize the 'I'.)

Now, to those who have ears to hear, this emphatic – this sovereign – 'I' of Christ's is infinitely suggestive of his self-awareness and the part he knew himself called to play in the saving ways of God with men. Six times this *ego* rings out in the Sermon on the Mount: 'You have heard that it was said (by Moses) to the men of old, but *I* say to you' (Matt. 5). Jesus speaks as if he were delivering a new *Torah*, a new law, a new revelation of God's nature and will for men. The same authoritative 'I' resounds polemically in his reply to the scribes who had explained his cure of demoniacs by the hypothesis of 'black magic' – collusion with the devil. 'It is by the finger of God that *I* cast out demons' (Luke 11.20). The same sovereign 'I' speaks with compassion in his great invitation to his law-burdened hearers: 'Come to *me*, all who labour and are heavy laden, and *I* will give you rest' (Matt. 11.28).

Alongside these sayings from the Synoptic Gospels (where there are more of them) we may set the great 'I am's' in St John's gospel, where, as Browning put it, the 'points' in the earlier gospels become 'stars' in the fourth. 'I am the bread of life' (6.35). 'I am the light of the world' (8.12). 'I am the resurrection and the life' (11.25). 'I am the true and living way' (to the Father, 14.6). 'I am the true Vine' (i.e. the true Israel, 15.1). Couched though these are in St John's own idiom and shot through with the light of the resurrection, they are true to the mind of Christ, for they make explicit claims which Jesus made for himself before he finished his work on the cross. And all are summed up in the phrase found four times in John's gospel 'I am what I am' (8.24, 28, 58; 13.19). This *ego eimi*, with its echo of God's word to Moses in Ex. 3.14, sounds uncommonly like the accent of deity.

From Christ's 'I am's to his 'I came's is an easy transition. 'He that cometh' was another name for the Messiah, so that our Lord's 'I came's are pregnant with a sense of his divine sending and destiny. 'I came not to call the righteous but sinners' (Mark 2.17). 'I came to cast fire on the earth' (Luke 12.49. Jesus is the new Prometheus). 'I did not come to abolish the law and the prophets but to fulfil them' (Matt. 5.17). To which we may add from St John's gospel. 'For judgment I came into the world' (9.39). 'I came that they may have life and have it more abundantly' (10.10). 'I did not come to condemn the world but to save the world' (12.48).

No record of Christ's 'egoistic' sayings would be complete without mention of his 'totalitarian' claims for commitment to himself. 'He who receives you receives me, and he who receives me receives him who sent me' (Matt. 10.40). 'Everyone who acknowledges me before men, I will also acknowledge before my Father who is in heaven; but whoever denies me before men, I will also deny before my Father who is in heaven.' (Matt. 10.32.) 'Whoever rejects me rejects him that sent me' (Luke 10.16). Faith does not rest in Jesus but in the Father who sent him, and therefore to reject Jesus is to reject God. Here then speaks one who knows himself uniquely authorized by God, who knows himself to be 'God's apostle' to mankind. No wonder wise old 'Rabbi' Duncan declared: 'Christ either deceived mankind by conscious fraud, or he was himself deceived, or he was divine. There is no getting out of this trilemma.'[1]

II

'The Man for others' *par excellence* is how John Robinson thinks of Jesus. Yet from his own words he stands revealed as the egoist *par excellence*. How shall we explain this paradox? Why thus: Christ's egoism was for others' sake, an egoism which took him to the cross.

This was the end which crowned the work of the man for others, the thing God sent him into the world to do, the most selfless act of egoism in human history –

> I should not mind to die for them
> My own dear downs, my comrades true,
> But that great heart of Bethlehem.
> He died for men he never knew.[2]

'He hath given us rest by his sorrow and life by his death' wrote Bunyan in words which have found an echo in countless hearts. If this be egoism, it is divine egoism, and in the last act of the man for others we see not only altruism incarnate but the holy love of the almighty Father agonizing for us, even unto death, in the person of his Son, who comes back from the grave with unshadowed peace upon his lips and the promise that he will be with us 'to the end of time' (Matt. 28.20).

NOTES

1. John Duncan, *Colloquia Peripatetica*, 1870, p. 109.
2. Hilton Brown.

8

The Magnanimity of Christ

According to the Authorized version, Paul wrote to his converts: 'Let your moderation be known to all men' (Phil. 4.6). 'Moderation in all things' is no doubt a wise rule for living, as it was a virtue much prized by the ancient Greeks. But was Paul really saying a good word for their maxim *Mēden Agan* 'Nothing in excess', and deprecating, not to say dousing, all healthy enthusiasm?

The Greek word which he uses here occurs seven times in the New Testament, twice as a noun (*epieikeia*) and five times as an adjective (*epieikēs*). Paul talks of the *epieikeia* of Christ (II Cor. 10.1). Elsewhere it is a moral quality required of Christians (I Tim. 3.3; Titus 3.2). And *epieikēs* is one of several adjectives used by St James to describe 'the wisdom which is from above' (James 3.17). If 'moderation' is not a happy translation of *epieikeia*, what kind of man is he who deserves the epithet *epieikēs*?

Four centuries before the Christian era, Aristotle contrasted him with the rigid stickler for legalities, the severely-judging man. The man with *epieikeia* is the man who can make allowances and is content with less than his due. To show *epieikeia*, he said, is to 'pardon human failings, to look to the law-giver rather than to the law, to the spirit and not to the letter, to the intention and not to the act'. What an admirable definition! How near he comes to the Sermon on the Mount! Aristotle has given us the clue to the real meaning of our word.

Shakespeare, we are told, had 'small Latin and less Greek'. No matter: he too, like Aristotle, knew what *epieikeia* is. In what is perhaps the most Christian passage in his plays, Portia's speech to Shylock, he goes unerringly to the meaning of the New Testament word. 'Mercy,' she tells Shylock, 'becomes the throned monarch better than his crown', nay,

> It is an attribute of God himself
> An earthly power doth then show likest God's
> When mercy seasons justice.[1]

Epieikeia is 'mercy seasoning justice'. The man who has this lovely virtue knows how to relax justice and let mercy come breaking in. But how shall we translate the word into English? Matthew Arnold's 'sweet reasonableness' is too sugary. Ronald Knox's 'courtesy' hardly measures up to the word's meaning as we have explained it. Moffatt's 'forbearance' (adopted by the RSV) is better. But perhaps best of all is Anderson Scott's 'magnanimity' (favoured by the NEB in II Cor. 10.1 and Phil. 4.5). 'Magnanimity' means greatness of soul – the kind of spiritual nobility which, because it looks to the whole and not the part, to the intention and not the act, and remembers good rather than evil, ever 'seasons justice with mercy'.

II

'I appeal to you,' wrote Paul to the contentious Christians of Corinth 'by the gentleness and magnanimity of Christ' (II Cor. 10.1). Forty years later, Clement bishop of Rome, writing to the Corinthian Christians, reminded them that 'our Lord Jesus taught magnanimity and long-suffering' (I Clem. xiii.1). He not only taught it; he embodied it.

Go back first to the case of the strange exorcist related in the ninth chapter of Mark's gospel.

John, son of Zebedee, said to Jesus: 'Master, we saw a man casting out demons in your name, and we forbade him because he was not following us'. Jesus said, 'Do not forbid him; for no one who does a mighty work in my name will be able soon after to speak evil of me. For he that is not against us is for us (Mark 9.38-40). Here was a man, not one of the chosen twelve, doing beneficent work in the name of Jesus. 'Those who are not against us' said Jesus to his men, 'are on our side.' It is a timeless rebuke to all Christian exclusiveness, to all who would erect religious fences. God's action, says Jesus in effect, is not limited to the forms with which we are familiar. He often works by agents who have no orthodox Christian label, and wherever we find them, and however strange their guise, we are to welcome them as allies. This is the magnanimity of Jesus. Let his modern disciples learn from him.[2]

Or consider Jesus' word on the cross: 'Father, forgive them, for they know not what they do.' (Luke 23.34). Scholars have debated who 'they' were – the Jews who cried 'Crucify him!' or the Roman soldiers who executed the sentence. Since both had a hand in his crucifixion, perhaps Jesus meant both. In their ignorance Jews and Romans were, in Paul's phrase, 'crucifying the Lord of glory' (I Cor. 2.8) – committing the greatest crime in history. Yet both are held up before the face of the almighty Father in merciful entreaty. This is *epieikeia* incarnate; and down the centuries few words of Jesus have so touched the hearts of men and moved them, in their judging, to temper justice with mercy.

Yet perhaps the true nature of *epieikeia* is best seen in the story of Jesus and the Adulteress (John 8.1-11, AV).

It is the tale of a trap set for Jesus by the scribes and Pharisees. If Jesus sanctions the stoning of the adulteress, he usurps the power of Rome who alone could inflict capital punishment. If he forbids it, he contravenes the law of Moses which prescribed death for an adulteress (Lev. 20.10; Deut. 22.21f.). Jesus avoided the trap – by writing with his finger on the ground.

This writing (as T. W. Manson pointed out) accorded with the procedures of Roman Law. In a Roman court the presiding judge first wrote down the sentence on a tablet before getting up to read it out aloud. And thus did Jesus. By his action he said in effect, 'You are inviting me to play the judge in true Roman fashion. Very well, I will do so'. Stooping down, he pretended to write the sentence on the ground, after which he straightened up and read it out: 'Let him who is without sin among you be the first to throw a stone at her' (compare Deut. 17.7).

No wonder the accusers slunk away. It is a master-stroke of mercy seasoning justice. Jesus defeats the plotters by 'going through the motions' of passing sentence, but at the same time so wording it that it cannot be carried out. He does not condone the woman's sin, as witness his 'Go and sin no more', but neither does he condemn her.

This is *epieikeia* in unforgettable action. Jesus does not condone the woman's sin – this is our Lord's justice. He refuses to condemn the sinner – this is his mercy. And it is this delicate balancing of justice and mercy which makes this one of the imperishable stories about Jesus.

Robert Burns once wrote:

> Then gently scan your brother man,
> Still gentler sister woman,
> Though they may gang a kennin wrang,
> To step aside is human.[3]

But 'gentle scanning' of 'sister woman' is, by Jesus' judgment, also divine, even if Jesus does not 'step aside' – ignore the sin. Here is matter of thought for all Christians, and especially for those called to sit in judgment in one way or another on sinners. Is there not here a plain hint for all such Christian administrators of justice that the strictly legalistic administration of laws, however lofty the ideals they embody, is not, in the last resort, the best way of dealing with sinners as persons, more especially as not even the best of us is sinless? And whether we are called to sit on the judgment bench or not, are not all of us who profess to be Christians called, in our day-to-day dealings with our fellow-men, to season justice with mercy?

NOTES

1. *The Merchant of Venice*, Act IV, Sc. 1, 11.195f.

2. Is there not a flagrant contradiction between Mark 9.40 ('He that is not against us is for us') and Matt. 12.30, paralleled in Luke 11.23 ('He who is not with me is against me')? How are we to reconcile these two sayings of Jesus? By reference to their setting in his ministry. The negative one, Matt. 12.30, addressed to the *crowds*, demands unconditional decision for Jesus in that war between the kingdom of God and the kingdom of evil in which there can be no neutrals. The positive one, Mark 9.40, addressed to *disciples*, rebukes the censorious attitude of men who make of their discipleship their own personal privilege.

3. 'Address to the Unco Guid' (or 'Rigidly Righteous').

9

The Metaphors of the Master

'If I were asked what has been the most powerful force in the making of history,' wrote Macneile Dixon, 'I should answer: metaphor.'[1] Let us not dismiss this as the hyperbole of a modern man of letters. At his back Dixon has the ancient 'master of those who know.' 'The greatest thing by far is to have the command of metaphor,' said Aristotle, adding that, for its effective use, you must have 'an eye for resemblances'.

Nowadays we tend to misprize metaphor in a way that the Elizabethans (witness Shakespeare) never did. To us, metaphor appears as a happy extra trick of style. Yet, properly understood, it is a basic principle of language and the interchange of thoughts. Thinking is essentially metaphoric, as it mostly proceeds by noting resemblances and making comparisons. Almost all teaching, for example, consists in comparing the unknown with the known, the strange with the familiar. We can hardly explain anything except by saying that it is *like* something else, something more familiar and intelligible. This was perhaps the reason why the little girl, being asked which bits of the Bible she liked best, replied, 'the Like Sayings'.

Profoundly metaphoric was our Lord's thinking. To him, as an oriental, figurative speech came naturally. If John the Baptist was 'no reed bed swept by the wind' (Matt. 11.7), Herod Antipas was 'that fox' (Luke 13.32), Simon a 'rock' (Matt. 16.18), and James and John 'sons of thunder' (Mark 3.17). Though Jesus had never read Aristotle's *Poetics*, he had an unerring 'eye for resemblances' in the world over which God ruled as an almighty Father. Similes he liked. 'Be wise as serpents, and harmless as doves' (Matt. 10.16). 'I saw Satan fall like lightning from heaven' (Luke 10.18).

'How often have I longed to gather your children as a hen gathers her brood under her wings!' (Luke 13.34). So also, with a master's touch, he exploited metaphor (which is really compressed simile, with the 'like' or 'as' left out) in the service of that dawning divine kingdom which was the burden of all his words and works.

Literally, metaphor means 'transference', and it was Jesus' way, as he preached and taught the kingdom, to 'transfer' men's thinking from the natural to the spiritual world, as in his parables which are so often but expanded metaphors. One striking example, bearing on his Passion which we might better call his Action – the deed which consummated all he said and did – may introduce the other metaphors which we shall here discuss.

> I have come to set fire to the earth, and how I wish it were already kindled! I have a baptism to undergo, and how hampered I am until the ordeal is over! (Luke 12.49f.).

Fire and water! Our Lord, observe, has no qualms about 'mixing his metaphors' in order to describe his role as God's Prometheus sent to set the cathartic fire of the kingdom blazing in the world. It is a daring figure, this of himself as God's Incendiary, and a variation of it is preserved by Origen in one of the Lord's 'uncanonical sayings':

> He that is near me is near the fire,
> And he that is far from me is far from the Kingdom.

Metaphors, then, are woven into the woof and warp of Christ's thinking. For the most part, they are not those of the city-dweller, neither are they redolent of the rabbinical school. (Contrast St Paul's.) Farming and fishing, sowing and reaping, building and baking, the market-place and the eastern bazaar, the work of the shepherd, the ploughman, the physician – such are the activities, the places, the trades which provide the stuff of his metaphors – these, and of course the flowers of the field, the fish of the lake, and the birds of the air from the sparrow to the eagle.

And how masterfully he employs them to proclaim the kingdom, declare his Father's will, and pillory false religion! Was ever misguided fastidiousness in religion better described than as 'straining out a midge and swallowing a camel' (Matt. 23.24), or censoriousness more effectively rebuked than in, 'Why do you note the splinter in your

brother's eye and fail to see the plank in your own eye?'
(Matt. 7.3), or ostentatious piety more vividly forbidden
than in, 'When you do an act of charity, do not sound a
trumpet before you' (Matt. 6.2)? *Ex oriente lux!* In its un-
laboured simplicity, in its stress on 'the things which you
can touch and see', and in its pervading symbolism, Christ's
teaching comes to us prosaic occidentals with the piquancy
of foreign things and the refreshing sound of waters flowing
from eternal springs.

In a brief essay we cannot hope to mention all his metaphors. Let us concentrate on those in which Jesus speaks of
his person, describes the mission of his new Israel-to-be, and
shadows forth the purpose of that death which is to crown
his earthly ministry and inaugurate the coming of God's
kingdom 'in power' (Mark 9.1).

II

For a beginning, let us take a metaphor, hidden away in
the fifth chapter of John's gospel, which, like the splinter and
the plank, may well go back to the Nazareth workshop:

> Truly, truly I tell you, a son can do nothing by himself: he
> only does what his father is doing: what the father does the son
> does. For the father loves his son and shows him all he himself
> is doing (John 5.19f.).

Jesus has been accused by his Jewish critics of 'making
himself equal to his Father', which was a rabbinical phrase
to describe the action of a rebellious son. His reply is the
figure of the apprenticed son. Think, he says, of a son
apprenticed to his father's trade. (Such a family arrangement
was common enough in the simple society of Palestine.) He
does not hammer or chisel away on his own untutored impulse. Rather he watches his father at work (as the young
Jesus must have watched Joseph) and copies his every action.
And, in turn, the affectionate father initiates his son into
all the tricks of the trade. Just so, Jesus means, I imitate
my heavenly Father. By a homely metaphor he signals at
the last secret of his own spiritual life, his sense of unique
sonhood to his Father in heaven.

Consider next the figure of the *physician* which Jesus
applied to his ministry. Accused by the Scribes of consorting
with bad characters, he replies: 'It is not the healthy that

need a doctor but the sick' (Mark 2.17). Behind this saying lies the concept of sin as a *disease* which goes back to the prophets (e.g. Jer. 8.22; 17.9), and of himself as God's physician sent for its curing. 'He went about doing good', Peter was later to tell Cornelius and his friends at Caesarea, 'and healing all that were oppressed by the devil, for God was with him' (Acts 10.38). Still later he wrote to the Christians in Asia Minor, 'By his wounds you have been healed' (I Peter 2.24). 'What a new and strange method of healing,' said an early Christian commentator, 'the doctor suffered the cost, the sick received the healing.'

In the next paragraph of Mark's gospel the figure changes from physician to *bridegroom*. Reproached by the Pharisees for his disciples' failure to fast, Jesus replies that fasting would be as incongruous in that glad time (the dawning of the kingdom) as it would be at a marriage feast: 'Can you expect the bridegroom's friends to fast while the bridegroom is with them?' he asks, sombrely adding, 'but the time will come when the bridegroom will be taken away from them' (Mark 2.18-20). If here we recall the Baptist's little parable of the Bridegroom and the Best Man (John 2.29), we shall find in Jesus' reply a veiled claim to be the Messianic Bridegroom. Those who caught the drift of 'the nuptial metaphor' on Jesus' lips must have recalled Hosea's famous figure of Israel as the Bride of God and sensed a claim by Jesus to be Immanuel, God with us. It is the metaphor which later Paul employed to figure forth the spiritual union between Christ and his church (Eph. 5.25-33).

For Jesus a still fitter figure for his God-given work was that of *shepherd*. Centuries before prophets like Ezekiel and Micah had pictured the expected Messiah as God's shepherd and God's people as his flock (Ezek. 34.12, 16, 23; Micah 5.4). When we turn to the gospels, we find Jesus, in parable and saying, making veiled claim to be the Shepherd Messiah who gathers God's flock, goes out to seek and save the lost, and lays down his life not only for 'the lost sheep of Israel' but for others 'not belonging to this fold', so that there might be 'one flock, one shepherd' (Matt. 10.16; Mark 14.27f.; Luke 12.32; 15.3-6, and John 10.1-16).

This concept of Christ as God's Shepherd was quick to catch the Christian imagination – Peter calls him 'the Head Shepherd' (I Peter 5.4), and the writer to the Hebrews 'the great Shepherd of the sheep' (Heb. 13.20). And if you visit the catacombs of Rome, you find that the picture of Christ which the early Christians painted on the walls of their burial places was that of the Good Shepherd, as their prayer for the faithful departed was:

> Lord, let those who are asleep, when they are redeemed from death, freed from guilt, reconciled to the Father, and brought home on the shoulders of the Good Shepherd, enjoy everlasting blessedness.

The Apprenticed Son, the Good Physician, the Bridegroom of the true Israel, the great Shepherd of God's flock – by such metaphors Christ sought to convey the nature of his work, the purpose of his coming.

III

Now, beside them let us set four metaphors of his for those whom he designed to be the nucleus of his new People of God.

From 'halieutics' (the art of fishing) he drew his first one. Calling two pairs of brothers from their nets, he promised that henceforth they would 'catch' men (Mark 1.17; Luke 5.10). For the prophet Jeremiah (Jer. 16.16ff.), 'fishers of men' had meant God's ministers of judgment upon evildoers. For Jesus, the words described his disciples as messengers of salvation. They were called to 'hook' men for God and his kingdom (which, in a parable, he elsewhere compared to a seine net) 'Come with me,' he said, 'and I will turn you into fishers for men.'

For his next two metaphors we go to the Sermon on the Mount. 'You are the salt of the earth,' he told his chosen disciples (Matt. 5.13). It is on the preservative and purifying virtue of salt that the stress here falls. Applied to the disciples, it must mean their zeal and devotion by which God means to preserve the world from corruption. 'But if the salt become salt-less', he warns – if a Judas 'just for a handful of silver' turns traitor – there lies their danger.

From salt to light – 'You are the light of the world' (Matt. 5.14). What can light mean here but saving light – the light of that redeeming revelation, of which they were to be the bearers? The disciples were to act as *phosphori Dei* –

God's light-bringers. Centuries earlier Isaiah had described the mission of the Lord's Servant –

> I will give you as a light to the nations,
> That my salvation shall reach to the ends of the earth (Isa. 49.6).

Now, having kindled their torches at him who is 'the light of the world' (John 8.12), they were to be themselves light to lead men in a dark world to God's truth. It is the Galilean command to world-mission.

Salt and light are wholesome and radiant symbols which still today come home vividly to us when we try to suggest what a true Christian influence should be. But Christ's next metaphor ought to jerk us out of any temptation to be at ease in Zion. Somewhere, on the road to Jerusalem, Jesus told his hearers: 'If any man would come after me, let him deny himself and take up his cross and follow me' (Mark 8.34). To recapture the sinister ring of that figure requires real historical imagination. The first picture it evoked in his hearers' minds must have been the all too familiar one of the condemned criminal bearing the cross-beam (or transom) to the place of his execution. 'If you want to be loyal followers of mine', Jesus was saying, 'you must begin to live like men on their way to the gallows.'

We may seek to reassure ourselves by saying that this challenge was thrown out to men in a particular historical situation about AD 30. This is true. But can we, Christ's modern followers, thus easily close our ears to its challenge? Does it not epitomize, in one stark figure, what Dietrich Bonhoeffer called 'the *cost* of discipleship' and remind us that, as the disciple is not above his master, so no life today can be truly Christian which has in it no element of self-sacrifice for others' sake? Let people say what they will, wrote Von Hügel, there is no symbol so deeply comprehensive of our august religion as a *crucifix*.[2]

IV

Thus, finally, we reach the metaphors which Jesus used to shadow forth the end of all his ministry – those of the 'baptism', the 'cup' and the 'ransom'.

'I have a baptism to undergo,' he said in a metaphor already noted (Luke 12.49; Mark 10.38). Before God's Prometheus

can set the holy fire blazing in the world, there must come
for him his own baptism of blood. 'How hampered I am,' he
says, 'until the ordeal is over!' The saying not only hints
at his own spiritual travail but also suggests that his 'ordeal'
will serve as a gateway to a fuller and freer activity beyond
death when he will be 'let loose in the world where neither
Roman nor Jew can stop his truth'. (It is the same point which
Jesus makes in his little parable about the grain of wheat
which must die if it is to become greatly fruitful, John 12.24.)

In the second place, Jesus saw his Passion as a 'cup' which
God had given him to drink (Mark 10.38; 14.36). This metaphor goes back to the Old Testament where 'the cup of the
Lord' signifies not only suffering but even punishment which
is divinely ordained – compare Isa. 51.22 where God speaks
of 'the chalice of my wrath'. Was not this the 'cup' which
Jesus had in mind on the road to Jerusalem and in the
Garden? What wrung from him in Gethsemane the prayer
that 'if it were possible the hour might pass from him,' and
made him say, 'My heart is ready to break with grief,' was
not the mere prospect of physical pain but the anticipation
of that experience when the Father would put into his hands
the cup men's sins had mingled. So closely had he identified
himself with those he came to save that he had to experience,
in all its horror, the reaction of God's holy love against the
sin of man. Only such an explanation does justice to the
agony in the Garden and that later cry of dereliction (Mark
15.34) ineffably instinct with Jesus' feeling of descent into
that hell of utter separation from his Father: 'My God, my
God, why hast thou forsaken me?' 'I have sometimes thought,'
wrote T. R. Glover,[3] 'that there never was an utterance that
reveals more amazingly the difference between feeling and
fact. That was how Jesus felt. ... We feel that God was more
there than ever.'

Lastly, Jesus used the metaphor of a 'ransom' to describe
the purpose of his death. 'The Son of man came not to be
served but to serve and to give his life as a ransom for many
(Mark 10.45). His words are redolent of Isa. 53. 'To serve'
means to fulfil the mission of the Lord's Servant by whose
stripes sinners would be healed. 'To give his life as a ransom'
reflects the Hebrew of Isa. 53.10. 'For many' (which is Hebrew
'for all') echoes Isa. 53.11f.

What light does this metaphor shed on Jesus' thought

about his death? The least his words can mean is that the suffering Son of man lays down his life vicariously that others may be delivered. But it is not unduly pressing Jesus' words to say that by reason of their sins the lives of the 'many' had become forfeit, and that Jesus knew himself, as the Messianic Servant of the Lord, called to release them, by his sacrifice, from the doom which overhung them. 'Truly,' the Psalmist had written, 'no man can ransom himself or give to God the price of his life, for the ransom of his life is costly' (Ps. 49.7f.). What the 'many' cannot do for themselves, Jesus, by his vicarious and redemptive suffering, will do for them. The sacrifice of the innocent one will exempt the guilty.

Because he takes the saying seriously and, at the same time, preserves the mystery of –

> Desperate tides of the whole great world's anguish
> Forced through the channels of a single heart –

James Denney[4] is our best commentator here:

> If we feel that such a metaphor carries us out of our depth, that, as the words fall on our minds, we hear the plunge of the lead in fathomless waters, we shall not for that imagine that we have lost our way. By these things men live, and wholly therein is the life of the spirit. We cast ourselves on them because they outgo us; in their very immensity we are assured that God is in them.

So Jesus finished the work God had given him to do (John 19.30). And so God made the master of metaphor, who had called himself his apprenticed Son, into the world's redeemer.

NOTES

1. W. Macneile Dixon, *The Human Situation*, 1937, p. 65.
2. Friedrich von Hügel, *Letters to a Niece*, 1928, p. 94.
3. *The Jesus of History*, (1917) 1948 edition, p. 153.
4. *The Death of Christ*, Tyndale 1951, p. 45.

10

The Rule of Three

Strangely satisfying to men down the centuries has been the number three – and the idea of three-foldness. Did not Greek and Roman mythology suppose the world to be under the rule of three gods – Jupiter (heaven), Neptune (sea) and Pluto (hades) – as for the ancients both the Fates and the Furies were three. 'Three,' opined Pythagoras the Greek philosopher, 'is the perfect number, expressing beginning, middle and end', and so a symbol of deity. For Horace a heart encased in *aes triplex* 'triple brass' meant invincible courage in a man. And the conquering Julius Caesar announced his victory in the Pontic campaign with three alliterative verbs, '*Veni, vidi, vici* – I came, I saw, I conquered.'

But no less than Greek and Roman biblical man felt the spell of the number and had a liking for triads. 'A three-fold cord is not quickly broken', declared the Preacher (Eccles. 4.12). 'So faith, hope, love abide, these three' (I Cor. 13.13) said St Paul, naming the Christian graces. According to St John the snares of 'the world' (i.e., human society as it organizes itself apart from God) were 'the lust of the flesh, the lust of the eyes and the pride of life' (I John 2.16), and when he named the witnesses to the truth of Christian doctrine, he wrote: 'There are three witnesses, the Spirit, the water and the blood; and these three agree' (I John 5.8). For the Seer of Patmos three was the number of heaven, epitomized in the *Trisagion* 'Holy, holy, holy is the Lord God Almighty who was, and is, and is to come' (Rev. 4.8).

To this very day the rule of three pervades our every-day speech. When we wish to describe the ordinary man in the street, we say 'Tom, Dick and Harry'. When we tell a story (if we are born north of the Cheviots) we begin, 'There was an Englishman, and an Irishman, and a Scotsman'.

I

But there was another to whom the number three seems to have been congenial. In a valuable article in *The Expository Times* for May 1964 Dr C. L. Mitton has bidden us note Christ's love of three-foldness, whether he was teaching his disciples in crisp aphorism, or in parable challenging the crowds to decision for the kingdom of God.

Study the gospels, and you find that his words, ideas, topics tend to take a three-fold pattern. 'Hand', 'foot' and 'eye' represent for him our most precious physical possessions (Mark 9.43-47). Care-ridden human beings ask three questions, 'What shall we eat? What shall we drink? What shall we wear?' (Matt. 6.13). The birds of the air 'neither sow, nor reap, nor gather into barns' (Matt. 6.36). And as 'rain, floods and gales brought-down the sand-built house (Matt. 7.25), so the gifts bestowed on the returning prodigal were a robe, a ring, and a pair of shoes (Luke 15.22).

Nor does this exhaust the evidence. When Jesus rounds on Simon the priggish Pharisee, his rebuke is three-fold: 'You gave me no water for my feet ... you gave me no kiss ... you did not anoint my head with oil' (Luke 7.45). When he condemns that love of titles which is born of spiritual pride, he says:

> You must not be called 'rabbi', for you have one Rabbi, and you are all brothers;
> Do not call any man on earth 'father'; for you have one Father, and he is in heaven.
> Nor must you be called 'teacher'; you have one Teacher, the Messiah (Matt. 23.8-10, NEB).

And when he teaches his disciples the need to persevere in prayer, the rule of three marks both stanzas:

> Ask, and it shall be given you,
> Seek, and you will find,
> Knock, and it will be opened to you.
> For every one who asks receives,
> And he who seeks finds,
> And to him who knocks it will be opened (Matt. 7.7f.).

Scholars have noted that in his parables Jesus followed those rules for telling a story which men have found by long experience produce the most dramatic effect. One is the 'rule of contrast' whereby wisdom and folly, virtue and vice, riches and poverty are contrasted (e.g., Dives and Lazarus, the Wise and the Foolish Bridesmaids). Another is the 'rule of end stress' whereby the spotlight falls on the last act or person in the story (e.g., 'the barren rascal' in the Talents, the sending of the only son in the tale about the Wicked Tenants). But no less prominent is the 'rule of three' whereby the story has three main characters, like the three excusemakers in The Great Supper, the three servants in The Talents, the Priest, the Levite and the Samaritan on the Jericho Road, and the father and his two so different sons in the greatest parable of all.

II

It is well known that St Matthew had a penchant for grouping his materials in threes (as also in sevens) – three angelic messages to Joseph, three denials by Peter, three questions by Pontius Pilate. Is it then possible that the three-foldness we have been uncovering in the record of Christ's teaching is due not to him but to the evangelists or the men who shaped the oral tradition underlying the gospels?

This is improbable. In the Synoptic Gospels we find some sixty examples of triplicity in Christ's sayings. Now, as literary criticism has shown, underlying the first three gospels are four main sources: Mark, 'Q' (the non-Markan sayings of Jesus common to Matthew and Luke), 'M' (the matter peculiar to Matthew) and 'L' (the matter peculiar to Luke). Study these sources, and you will find three-foldness in all four. On a rough reckoning Mark yields fourteen examples, M ten, L seventeen and Q nineteen. Because all four gospel sources exhibit this three-foldness, it must go back to Jesus himself and form an original feature of his teaching style – as characteristic and authentic as, say, his habit of prefacing a momentous saying with the words 'Amen I tell you'. If Jesus knew that 'truth embodied in a tale' will fix itself in men's minds as no abstract argument ever will, he knew also that a three-fold form imparted to a saying or a parable would make it still more memorable.

III

One last reflection. A comparison of St Matthew and St

Luke will show that occasionally they reduced an original three items in a saying to two (perhaps because they had to shorten their materials to fit the length of a papyrus roll). Compare, for instance, Mark 9.43-47 which lists 'hand' 'foot' and 'eye' with Matt. 18.8 where the same saying of Jesus refers only to 'hand' and 'foot'. This makes it probable that when, in the same subject matter, St Matthew or St Luke has three items and the other only two, the three-fold form has strong claim to be original. Thus if St Matthew lists the destroyers of earthly treasures as 'moth' 'worm' and 'thieves' (Matt. 6.19f.), he probably preserves the words of Jesus more faithfully than St Luke who mentions only 'moth' and 'thieves' (Luke 12.33).

Occasionally we may, with probability, surmise an original three-foldness in Jesus' teaching where the evangelists fail to report it. An excellent example is the little parable of The Asking Son (Matt. 7.9f.; Luke 11.11f.). Common to both versions of the parable are 'fish' and 'serpent'. But, whereas Matthew has 'loaf' and 'stone', Luke has 'egg' and 'scorpion'. Because bread, fish and eggs were the three staple foods of Palestine, it is likely that Jesus in his parable referred to all three:

> What man of you, if his son asks him for a loaf, will give him a stone?
> Or if he asks for a fish, will give him a serpent?
> Or if he asks for an egg, will give him a scorpion?
> If you then, who are evil, know how to give good gifts to your children, how much more will your heavenly Father give good things to those who ask him!

The argument is: 'No human father, bad as he may be, would play such a scurvy trick as this on his son. How much less, then, the all-good Father above!'

We say three is a lucky number. It is more: it is a dominical one. (Jesus did not believe in 'luck' but in an all-wise heavenly Father.) Preachers who go in for what are called 'three-decker' sermons are often the targets for light banter. Yet in so doing they not only appeal to man's immemorial love of triplicity; they copy the style of him who 'spoke as never man spoke'.

The Great Thanksgiving
Matt. 11.25-30

Jubelruf 'shout of joy' the Germans call these words of Jesus, doubtless because St Luke introduced them with the words, 'At that moment Jesus exulted in the Holy Spirit'. Our English name for them is 'the Great Thanksgiving'. There are no verses in the first three gospels more important.

Discussing them in 1927, Claude Montefiore candidly confessed that, as a Jew, he would like to prove that Jesus never uttered these words, because, if it could be shown that he did, orthodox Christianity would have received notable support. This he thought unlikely and went on to prophesy that, as the years went by, the voices raised in support of their authenticity, would grow fewer and feebler.

Has his prophesy been fulfilled?

To begin with, let us note that Matt. 11.25-30 has three strophes, or stanzas, each with the marks of Hebrew poetry upon it. The first two – 11.25-26 and 11.27 – make up 'the Great Thanksgiving' and are closely paralleled in Luke 10.21-22. The third strophe – Matt. 11.28-30 – commonly called 'the Great Invitation' – has no such parallel. Some scholars think it stood, along with the first two strophes, in Q, that collection of our Lord's sayings used as a primary source by St Matthew and St Luke. Others think that St Matthew drew it from his own special source, usually called M. Whatever be the truth, the question is whether all three strophes preserve authentic words of Jesus.

I

Strophe I: Matt. 11.25f. (Luke 10.21)

I thank thee, Father, Lord of heaven and earth.
That thou hast hidden these things from the wise and clever,
And hast revealed them to the simple,
Yes, Father, for such was thy gracious will.

Everything favours the authenticity of this strophe – its clear poetic structure, its echoes of the Old Testament (e.g., Ps. 19.7 'making wise the simple'), the word 'Father' concealing an original Aramaic *Abba* (Jesus' unique form of address to God), the apparent harshness of his 'Thank God for their unbelief,' the congruency of the whole verse with the known course of his ministry.

What is uncertain is its place in that ministry. St Matthew locates it in the midst of the Galilean ministry, after his 'Woes' on the Galilean cities. St Luke attaches it to the joyful return of the seventy from their mission, where certainly it seems better placed. But some scholars have surmised that the words were spoken after Caesarea Philippi when increasing evidence of the disciples' growing faith may have moved Jesus to draw back a corner of the veil which hid the last secret of his own spiritual life.

Whatever their original setting, 'these things' concealed by the Father from 'the wise and clever' must refer to the dawning of God's kingdom which was the burden of all Jesus' preaching and teaching. And since it was to the disciples only that Jesus spoke of his knowledge of Abba Father, 'these things' may well refer to the secret of his own unique sonship. This gives an excellent connexion between Strophes I and II.

The first strophe's meaning is clear. As 'the wise and clever' (Isa. 29.14) are the Scribes, the official custodians of Israel's wisdom, so the 'simple' are the child-like to whom the kingdom belongs (Mark 10.18f.; Matt. 18.3), i.e., the disciples. Not to the sophisticated but to the simple – not to those proudly sure of their title to 'the very shape of knowledge and truth' (Rom. 2.20), but to those unskilled as babes in scribal lore – has Christ's doctrine come as the divine revelation which it is. But in this apparent miscarriage Jesus discerns the gracious purpose of the almighty Father.

If he gives thanks for the Scribes' unbelief, this is a Semitic way of speaking. We in the West might have said that, in the providence of God, pride of knowledge had brought its own nemesis. Moreover, a revelation accessible to 'babes' must be accessible to all – even Scribes, if they are prepared to 'become as little children'. We know of one proud pupil of Gamaliel who did so and helped to change the course of history.

II

Strophe II: (Matt. 11.27; Luke 10.20)

All things have been delivered to me by my Father:
And no one knows the Son but the Father;
Neither does any know the Father but the Son,
And any one to whom the Son chooses to reveal him.

There is a natural connexion between this strophe and the preceding one. Strophe I gives thanks for the revelation and its recipients, not the wise but the simple. Strophe II declares the way by which the revelation comes – from the Father through the Son.

But read Strophe II again, let its staggering claim come home to you, and you will perhaps understand why, half a century ago, the radical critics of Germany refused to believe that these could be genuine words of Jesus. The reasons for their scepticism were three:

(1) Jesus (and certainly not the 'reduced' Jesus of Liberal Protestantism) could not have made the absolute claim contained in this verse.

(2) Its 'Johannine' ring gives it away as surely as Peter's 'north country' accent gave him away on a historic occasion.

(3) It is really 'a Hellenistic revelation word' (Bultmann) without rootage in Palestine, let alone in the mind of Jesus.

How unconvincing these three reasons now appear!

A parallel to the Father-Son usage of this verse occurs in Mark 13.32 whose authenticity none but the most hardened sceptic would dispute. And there is ample evidence elsewhere in the synoptic tradition (Luke 2.49; Matt. 16.17; Mark 1.11; 12.6 plus, above all, Jesus' unique invocation of God as Abba) to make it entirely credible that Jesus could have styled himself 'the Son' *simpliciter*. This verse but sets the capstone on what has been called 'the divine consciousness of Jesus' which is writ so large elsewhere in the gospels.

Nor does the second charge stand up any better. That the verse resembles certain sayings in John's gospel is not to be denied. But this is no reason for condemning it unless we make it a canon of criticism that any saying in the Synoptic Gospels with parallels in John's must *ipso facto* be inauthentic. Precisely the opposite must now be argued.

Deep-rooted in what is now generally admitted to be the *independent* tradition of John's gospel is Jesus' sense of unique sonship to the Father. Once it occurs in the little parable of the Apprenticed Son (John 5.19f.), and thrice in explicit sayings of Jesus. 'The Father loves the Son and has given all things into his hands' (John 3.35). 'The Father knows me and I know the Father' (John 10.15). 'No one comes to the Father but by me' (John 14.6).

Finally, it is no longer permissible to pronounce the verse 'a Hellenistic revelation word'. The Hellenistic parallels produced were never impressive, and in recent years the discovery of the Dead Sea Scrolls has altered the whole picture. So large a place does 'knowledge' play in the Scrolls that it is unnecessary to go outside Palestine to account for the language of this verse. Not Hellenism but Hosea (a book well known to Jesus) – not pagan *gnōsis* but that 'knowledge of God' found in the Old Testament prophets and the Scrolls – supplies the likeliest background to the supreme 'I-Thou' relationship described in our passage.

We conclude that Matt. 11.27 is a genuine saying of Jesus.

Now for its interpretation: What does Jesus mean when he says that 'all things' have been 'delivered' to him by his Father? Not 'all power', for since Jesus was not yet glorified (John 7.29), the idea of universal power (Matt. 28.18) is not relevant. The natural meaning is 'all knowledge' – all the revelation needed for his mission. For (1) Jesus proceeds to speak, and speak exclusively, of the knowledge of God, and (2) the verb 'delivered' (Greek, *paredothē*) suggests a contrast with the 'tradition' (*paradosis*, Mark 7.8) of the Scribes whom he clearly has in mind. Their 'tradition', or 'handing down', was from man to man, rabbi to rabbi. Here it is from God to Jesus. Accordingly, 'all things' must mean here the complete revelation of God's saving purpose. 'All I need for my task,' Jesus says, 'has been shown me by my Father.'

The next two clauses show why Jesus is qualified to reveal that purpose. His competence, he says, springs from an exclusive and reciprocal relationship between the Father and himself, the Son:

> No one knows the Son but the Father,
> Neither does any know the Father but the Son.

The order of the clauses answers to the Old Testament

concept of the knowledge of God. In the prophets' view, if man is to know God, God must first know man. And it is because of the Father's prior knowledge of him, that Jesus claims he knows the Father as no other does. Here of course we are in the realm of ultimate mystery. The secret of the Father remains with the Son. No man knew, or knows, why God chose Jesus of Nazareth.

Even so, we need not doubt what Jesus meant by 'knowing God', and it is not to Hellenism but to the Old Testament that we must look for the answer. What is meant is not theological expertise but heart-to-heart communion, a personal 'I-Thou' relation, engaging heart and mind and will, initiated and sustained by the Father, and complemented and fulfilled by Jesus' own filial response of obedient love, something writ large in the gospels from the wilderness temptation to the agony in Gethsemane.

Finally, unique though his communion with the Father is, Jesus declares it is one into which he can lead others:

> And anyone to whom the Son chooses to reveal him.

In Strophe II therefore Jesus claims that he is both to God and man what no other can be. He is the Son who alone knows the Father, and he is the mediator through whom alone this personal knowledge of the Father comes to men. He is 'the true and living way' to the unseen Father, and there is no other.

IV

Strophe III: Matt. 11.28-30 only

> Come to me, all you who labour and are heavy laden,
> And I will give you rest.
> Take my yoke upon you, and learn from me,
> For I am gentle and lowly in heart,
> And you will find rest for your souls.
> For my yoke is easy, and my burden is light.

Two questions arise here. First, are these authentic words of Jesus? And, second, if they are, do they connect naturally with the two strophes of the Great Thanksgiving?

(1) Even if the Great Invitation did not stand in Q but came from M, this is no disproof of its authenticity. No one makes it a count against their genuineness that parables like

The Labourers in the Vineyard or The Talents come from Matthew's special source. No more should its derivation from M (if that be the truth) be an argument against the authenticity of the Great Invitation. On the contrary, much in its form and content argue it 'dominical':

First, it has the *Kina* (dirge) rhythm commonly found in passages of our Lord's teaching marked by strong emotion (like his lament over Jerusalem).[1]

Second, the promise of 'rest' to the 'heavy laden' is entirely in the spirit of one who condemned the scribes for 'loading men with burdens hard to bear' (Luke 12.26; Matt. 23.4).

Third, the self-description 'I am gentle and lowly in heart' echoes that of the Lord's Servant in Isa. 42.2f. and 53.1ff., and is apparently confirmed in II Cor. 10.1 where Paul appeals to 'the meekness and gentleness of Christ' as to a well-known trait in his character.

In the light of such evidence it becomes hard to believe that the strophe does not preserve words of Jesus. For myself, I should agree with Walter Pater (when discussing Christianity with the sceptical George Eliot): 'You think,' he said to her, 'that the Christian religion is all plain ... I don't. Take that saying of Jesus "Come unto me, all ye that labour and are heavy laden, and I will give you rest." There is mystery in that.' In short, if I have to choose between regarding the Great Invitation as a 'community creation' and a genuine saying of Jesus, my decision is not in doubt. Communities do not create great sayings like this.

(2) Does the Great Invitation fit naturally into the place which St Matthew assigns it after the Great Thanksgiving? Most certainly it does. In the Thanksgiving the first thought is for the revelation itself, and then the revelation is said to be mediated by the Son. So, in the Invitation, there comes first a general offer of 'rest', and then the 'rest' is said to be had by the acceptance of Jesus' 'yoke'. William Manson put the point well: 'because Jesus is the revealer of God in his teaching, he holds the secret of life and peace for all who turn to him.'[2]

If then the Great Invitation goes back to Jesus, what does it mean?

Those who first heard it may have found it faintly familiar. It recalled words from a book written in Hebrew two centuries earlier in Jerusalem which had become a prime favourite with the Jews, Ecclesiasticus, 'the gem among the

Apocrypha'. In his last chapter the author Ben Sira, assuming the role of personified Wisdom, invites the unlearned to '*come*' to him and 'lodge in his house of *learning*', to 'put their necks under the *yoke*, and let their souls receive instruction', and so, like himself, 'find much *rest*' (Ecclus. 57.23-27).

What is this 'yoke' of Ben Sira's? For him, 'wisdom' means the Jewish Law. It is the yoke of the Law as interpreted by the Scribes. Devoted study of it, he says, will bring man peace of mind.

In the Great Invitation to those who are 'weary and heavy laden' under that Law's burdens, Jesus proposes *a change of yokes*. What Ben Sira says about the Law he transfers to God's new order, the kingdom now dawning in his person and work. 'Take my yoke upon you,' he invites, 'and learn from me.' As his yoke is that of the new kingdom, so to 'learn' from Jesus is to learn how to serve God and man in that realm over which Abba Father rules. In discipleship to him (which is equivalent to entering the kingdom) they will 'find rest for their souls'. For he, God's apostle to men, is 'gentle and lowly in heart', as the yoke he offers is 'easy' (kindly) and the 'burden' he imposes 'light' (because 'lined with love,' said Matthew Henry).

Thus the Invitation carries a contrast between the Scribes' yoke of legal religion and Christ's new yoke in that kingdom where the king is a Father and whose 'royal law' is love. And the promise is that he who 'comes' to Jesus – enters the kingdom – will have access to the Father, an access which is the gracious gift of God's Son and his mediator to men.

It is a promise whose truth was validated in the experience of Christ's great apostle. Writing to the Roman Christians, Paul told how, when he quite despaired of fulfilling the Law's demands, he found rescue and rest by accepting the Great Invitation (Rom. 7.13-25). Through Christ Paul found the longed-for new relationship with God – one of sonship, not of slavery – because through the Son he gained access to the Father. And if it involved a new law – 'the law of Christ' (Gal. 6.2) – this law, by his own testimony, was no 'burden' because he had put his neck under Christ's yoke and in union with him 'had strength for anything' (Phil. 4.13).

Has not this been the deepest secret of the Christian life down nineteen centuries? Horatius Bonar, prince of Scottish hymn-writers, speaks for all the initiated:

> I heard the voice of Jesus say,
> Come unto me and rest,
> Lay down, thou weary one, lay down
> Thy head upon my breast:
> I came to Jesus as I was,
> Weary and worn and sad,
> I found in him a resting-place,
> And he has made me glad.

NOTES

1. C. F. Burney, *The Poetry of Our Lord*, 1925, pp. 144f.
2. *Jesus the Messiah*, 1943, p. 73.

12

'And the Word was God'

Like a little learning, a little Greek may be a dangerous thing. *Theos* is Greek for 'God'; but when the New Testament writers (who, except for Luke, were Jews) refer to God, they generally write *ho theos* 'the God' i.e., the only true God. This point was evidently unknown to the Jehovah's Witness who categorically assured the Scotswoman that the true meaning of John 1.1 was not, as the Authorised Version says, 'and the Word was God' but 'the Word was a god'. (Here we may observe that the Witnesses hold very 'reduced' views of Christ's person.)

Why is the Jehovah's Witness wrong and the AV (followed by the RV, the RSV and the Jerusalem Bible) right in the rendering of John 1.1?

Look again at the verse. 'In the beginning was the Word, and the Word was with God (*pros ton theon*), and the Word was God.' The Greek for the last five words is: *Theos ēn ho Logos*. But the omission of the definite article here before *theos* does not entitle us to translate 'And the Word was a god'. Supporting the AV's 'And the Word was God' are (1) Greek grammar (2) the context and (3) John's theology.

E. C. Colwell, an acknowledged American expert on New Testament Greek, has given his name to what is called 'Colwell's rule'. After careful study of New Testament usage, he laid down the rule that 'a definite predicative nominative has the definite article when it follows the verb, but that when it precedes it it does not'. Since in John 1.1 the predicative nominative *theos* precedes the verb, we should translate 'the Word was God', not 'the Word was a god'.

Now study the context. The Greek of John 1.1 cannot mean 'the Word was a god'. This would suggest that *theos* was a generic concept like *anthrōpos* ('man'), so that there could be two divine beings, in a polytheistic sense. Why is this meaning impossible here? Because in the immediately preceding sentence 'the Word was with God', *theos* with the article prefixed has its usual Jewish monotheistic sense.

Finally, consider John's theology. Turn from John 1.1 to John 20.28 and Doubting Thomas's confession. 'My Lord and my God' is his cry in the hour of his conversion from scepticism. The wheel of the gospel has come full circle: the note struck at the gospel's beginning rings out again near its ending.

Thus the traditional rendering of John 1.1 accords with John's theology. As long ago Bishop Westcott observed, the word-order of John 1.1 is deliberate. By his phrasing St John never intended to ascribe inferiority of nature to the *Logos* or Word (as the Jehovah's Witness would have had the woman believe): his sole concern was to 'avow the true deity of the Word'.

What is our conclusion? The Watch Tower's translation stands condemned. Moffatt's 'the Word was divine' is inadequate. (Had St John meant just this, he would have written *theios* 'divine', an adjective found in Acts 17.29 and II Peter 1.3.) Excellent is the New English Bible's 'What God was the Word was'. But there is no sound reason for departing from the Authorised Version's 'And the Word was God'.

The moral of it all? A reminder that, as Renan said, *la verité consiste dans les nuances* – and a warning against all Jehovah's Witnesses who, like their founder C. T. Russell, the Pennsylvanian haberdasher, are weak on Greek!

13

Pedilavium and Passion

John 13

A very remarkable true story[1] tells how, in 1901, by some
freak of time, two Oxford dons (Miss Moberly and Miss
Jourdain), walking in the grounds of the Palace of Versailles,
walked straight back into the year 1789 and saw Marie
Antoinette queen of France and others of that fateful time.
If some of us could thus escape into the past, it is not to
Versailles on the eve of the Revolution but to an upper
room in Jerusalem on an April evening in AD 30 that we
would go ...

I

It is Thursday night and the eve of the Jewish Passover.
Over the grey roofs of Jerusalem rides the Paschal moon.
Out in the streets of the Holy City all is quiet:

> Not a spark in the warren under the giant night,
> Save where in a turret's lantern beamed a grave, still
> light;
> There in the topmost chamber, a gold-eyed lamp was
> lit –
> Marvellous light in darkness, informing, redeeming it.
>
> For, set in that tiny chamber, Jesus the blessed and the
> doomed,
> Spoke to the lone disciples, as light to men entombed;
> And, spreading his hands in blessing, as one soon to be
> dead,
> He put soft enchantment into spare wine and bread.
>
> He smiled subduedly, telling, in tones soft as the voice
> of the dove,
> The endlessness of sorrow, the eternal solace of love;

And lifting the earthly tokens, wine and sorrowful bread,
He bade them sup and remember One who lived and was
dead.

And they could not restrain their weeping. But one rose
up to depart,
Having weakness, and hate of weakness, raging within
his heart,
And bowed to the robed assembly whose eyes gleamed
wet in the light.
Judas arose and departed: night went out to the night.

But our poet Robert Nichols has omitted one episode
recorded only by St John – the *pedilavium*, or washing of the
disciples' feet.

The supper had begun – that supper to which all our
Lord's suppers run back – when contention arose among the
disciples about who should be the greatest (Luke 22.24-27).
Think of it – Jesus presently going out to death and his
disciples are still blinded by visions of thrones and crowns!
Silently Jesus arises, puts off his coat, procures a basin, ties
a towel around him, and is down on his knees washing his
disciples' feet. The Son of God has 'taken the form of a
servant' (Phil. 2.7), the Servant of the Lord.

Now, with towel and basin, he is at the feet of Judas –
Judas who will soon be slipping out to finish his black
treachery. Now he moves round to Peter who, in horror,
draws up his feet: 'You, Lord, washing my feet?' Jesus
answers: 'You do not understand what I am now doing, but
one day you will.' 'You shall never wash my feet!' replies
Peter. 'If I do not wash you,' says Jesus, 'you will have no
share with me in my glory.'[2] The deeper truth begins to dawn
on Peter, and he goes to the opposite extreme. 'Then, Lord,'
he cries, 'Not my feet only. My hands and head as well!
Wash me all over.' Jesus answers: 'A man who has bathed[3]
needs no further washing; he is altogether clean, and you
are clean, though (referring to Judas) not every one of you.'

The foot-washing over, Jesus, assuming his garments, takes
his place again at the table's head. 'Do you understand,' he
asks, 'what I have done for you? If I, your Lord and Master,
have washed your feet, you also ought to wash one another's
feet. For I have given you an example, that you also should
do as I have done to you.'

As the supper proceeds, Jesus becomes deeply agitated.

'Truly, truly, I tell you,' he says, 'one of you is going to betray me.' The disciples are perplexed and dismayed. Whom can he mean? Then Peter nods to the Beloved Disciple reclining close to Jesus: 'Ask him who it is.' 'It is he,' says Jesus, 'to whom I give this bread after I have dipped it in the dish.' He hands the sop to Judas, the man of Kerioth, purse-bearer to the twelve. And Judas, having taken it, goes out. As the door closes, there comes a brief glimpse of the murk outside. 'And it was night.' Are there four more dramatic mono-syllables in literature? Judas was going out from 'the light of the world' into outer darkness.

With the traitor gone, the spirit of Jesus rises again, and in solemn triumph he cries, 'Now is the Son of man glorified'. So he tells them of the cross in which God will display his full glory in the Son of man. Then, remembering the wrangling disciples, he gives them his new commandment: 'As I have loved you, so you also are to love one another. By this shall all men know that you are my disciples, if you have love for one another.'

He is going home, home to his Father. 'Where I am going,' he tells them, 'you cannot follow me now, but one day you will.' 'Why not?' protests Peter, impulsive as ever, 'I will lay down my life for you.' 'Will you indeed, Peter?' says Jesus sadly, 'Ah Peter, Peter, before cockcrow you will have denied me three times.'

II

It is a wonderful chapter in the profoundest of the gospels. Yet there is *mystery* in it, especially in that dialogue between Jesus and Peter (vv. 6-10). What does Jesus really mean when he says to Peter, 'If I wash thee not, thou hast no share with me'?

Mystified by that conversation between Peter and his Master, many go straight on to vv. 12-15 (the call to service) and take the whole episode to be an acted parable whose theme is the glory of humble service. Beyond doubt, lowly, loving service is part of the lesson Jesus would teach his disciples. But to reduce the whole episode to an acted parable with a moral lesson is to miss half its truth and make of that dialogue between Peter and Jesus an intrusive irrelevance in which Jesus merely darkens counsel with words.

Study it yet again, and you will find something much deeper. Remember, first, its setting – all is enacted within the shadow of the cross – that cross which earlier Jesus had called his 'baptism' – his baptism in blood (Mark 10.38; Luke 12.49) – and that Jesus is the Servant Messiah soon to 'give his life as a ransom for many' (Mark 10.45). Next, note the verbs which St John employs to describe Jesus' actions. Jesus 'lays down' (*tithēsin*) his garments and, the washing over, 'takes them again' (*lambanei*). They are the same verbs which 'the good shepherd' had used of his vicarious death and resurrection (John 10.17). Finally, recall that the motif of the whole story is *cleansing*.

Put these three things together – setting, verbs and motif – and the deeper meaning becomes clear. Like the double acted parable of the broken bread and outpoured wine, the foot-washing is a symbolic act foreshadowing the cross and offering the disciples a share in its purifying power. The point of Jesus' warning to Peter 'If I do not wash you, you have no share with me,' is that there is no place in the Christian fellowship, with its promise of glory, for those who have not been cleansed by the atoning death of Christ, proleptically symbolized in the foot-washing. *Pedilavium* and Passion belong together, and the one interprets the other.

Now Jesus' call to lowly service (vv. 12-15) is seen to be the corollary to the foot-washing. The lesson which Jesus reads the disciples in the upper room is the same as he had read them on the road to Jerusalem (Mark 10.32-45).[4] Because they are cleansed by the Servant Son of God, they must respond by serving others in lowly love. *Noblesse oblige!* Of course, when Jesus bids them wash one another's feet, it is the spirit – the moral essence – of his act and example, not the letter – which matters. Not crowns and coronets but towels and basins are the insignia of God's kingdom, and he best honours God's Servant Son who is prepared to stoop and serve.

III

What has the story to say to us?

Many people today are like Peter before he fully grasped his Master's 'If I do not wash you'. They would like to be Christians but see little significance in that end which crowned Christ's saving work. They are ready to admire his life and praise his moral teaching (however impracticable they may think it). But they feel no need for cleansing by that strange man upon his cross. Never have they come to that crisis of blessed despair which moved Dr Thomas Chalmers to cry, in his great simplicity, 'What could I do if God did not justify the ungodly?' What they cannot credit is that without that cross and its shining sequel they would still be in their sins. This is the 'scandal' of Christianity for modern man who believes he can save himself, and will not realize that this is the one thing he may never do, because he cannot cleanse his own evil heart which lies at the root of all his trouble.

Yet that 'scandal' – a Christ crucified and raised for our sins, and not for ours only but for a whole world's – is the heart of the apostolic gospel. Without it there is no 'good news' for guilty man. If Christ does not cleanse us by his 'blood' – his stainless life laid down in death for us – we are unredeemed. But, and if, by faith we apprehend that on the cross Christ bore our sins that for us there might be condemnation no more, then we know that 'we have been bought with a price', we want to cry with Peter, 'Lord, wash me all over' and, knowing this grace wherein we stand, we rejoice in hope of the glory of God.

NOTES

1. *An Adventure.*

2. The Greek *echein meros* in v. 8 can mean simply 'share with'; but *meros* probably means more than 'fellowship'. In the LXX it translates the Hebrew *hēleq* and means a 'share' or 'heritage' in the Promised Land. On Jesus' lips it will mean a share in his heavenly glory. See Raymond Brown, *The Gospel according to St John*, Geoffrey Chapman 1971, pp. 565f.

3. In v. 10 the NEB (and most modern scholars) prefer the shorter reading and regard 'except for his feet' as a scribe's later addition. In *Neotestamentica et Patristica* (1962) J. A. T. Robinson rightly sees that John 13.1-20 is John's equivalent of Mark 10.32-45. Jesus is going to glory – this is why the disciples call him 'Lord and Master'. But if they are to have a share in it, they must drink the cup he drinks and share the baptism. The disciple is not greater than his master. Jesus' glory is the glory of the Servant Messiah. Can the disciples accept this? This is the question posed by the conversation between Jesus and the disciples in Mark 10.32-45 and by Jesus' symbolic act in John 13.

There are good reasons for believing that the story of the footwashing (of which an echo survives in Luke 22.24-27 with its closing 'I am among you as one who serves') came from the same general reservoir of gospel tradition as many of the narratives in the Synoptic Gospels. See C. H. Dodd, *Historical Tradition in the Fourth Gospel*, Cambridge University Press 1963, p. 63.

14

The Eleventh Commandment
John 13.34

Some of us can never read John 13.34 without being reminded of Samuel Rutherford and the village of Anwoth, in Galloway, where in the seventeenth century he ministered to a beloved people:

> O if one soul from Anwoth
> Meet me at God's right hand,
> My heaven will be two heavens
> In Immanuel's land.

So sang Rutherford whose collected letters have been pronounced 'the most seraphic book in our literature'.

But these were the days when Presbyterians and Episcopalians strove bitterly with each other. One Saturday night, as he journeyed incognito through the unfriendly land, the great Archbishop Ussher knocked at the Anwoth manse door and was invited to stay the night.

Now on Saturday evenings it was Rutherford's custom to 'catechize' his household, and the stranger in their midst presently found himself being asked, 'How many commandments are there?' Judge of the family's horror when he answered, 'Eleven', and did not seem black ashamed of himself either.

Next morning, Rutherford rose early and went into a nearby grove to say his prayers. Imagine his surprise when he found the stranger there also, evidently bent on the same purpose. Thereupon Ussher made himself known and was promptly invited to take the morning service. But yet another surprise awaited Rutherford when Ussher gave out his text: 'A new commandment give I unto you, that ye love one another.' Then Rutherford, sitting next to his wife in the manse pew, leaned over and said to her, 'There you have it! The eleventh commandment!'

I

In this 'permissive age' many, like the Archbishop of Canterbury, Dr Coggan, believe that the 're-moralizing' of our society ought to begin with a return to the Ten Commandments. A salutary start might be made if such commandments as:

> You shall not commit murder
> You shall not commit adultery
> You shall not steal
> You shall not give false evidence against your neighbour

were to be made the basis of a 'moral re-armament' programme, for adults as well as children. There is much wisdom in the proposal, and we wish our new Christian moralists God-speed in their crusade.

Yet the Ten Commandments have one notable drawback. As the little American lass observed, 'They don't tell you what you ought to do' – and she added, 'They just put ideas into your head.' There the eleventh commandment differs from the first ten. They are negative; it is positive. It does 'tell you what you ought to do'. It tells you to 'love one another'.

But here we face a problem. Nowadays 'love' is a kind of verbal chameleon, which can cover almost everything from Hollywood to heaven. What does the New Testament – what did Jesus mean – by 'love'?

The Greek language has three chief words for 'love'. First comes *erōs*, or desire. This is the love which craves and, at its lowest, lusts. Not once is it found in the New Testament. Next comes *philia*, 'friendship' – mutual affection between kindred spirits like, say, David and Jonathan in the Old Testament. Once only (James 4.4) does it occur in the New Testament. Finally, there is *agapē*, and the New Testament resounds with it. *Agapē* is the love which seeks not to possess but to give. If *erōs* is all 'take', and *philia* is 'give and take' *agapē* is all 'give'. This is Christ's word for love, and this the verb used in the eleventh commandment.

For Jesus, 'love' does not mean sex or sentimentalism.

Study his teaching about it in his great Sermon (Matt. 5.43-48; Luke 6.27f.) or in parables like those of the Good Samaritan and the Last Judgment, and note how practically and all-embracingly he defines the verb to 'love'. By 'loving' he means 'caring' – caring actively and selflessly, not merely for the decent and deserving but, as the parable of the Last Judgment teaches, for all in need of help. Even those we count our enemies, he says, must be included in our love's outreach, for there must be no limit to our loving as our heavenly Father's love knows no bounds (Matt. 5.44-48 NEB). 'How can I love my neighbour when I don't know who he is?' asked the 'lawyer' in that famous story about the Jericho Road. Jesus answered, 'Real love never asks questions like this. It knows no bounds of race. All it asks for is opportunities of going into action.'

II

Yet this is only half of love's story in the New Testament. If in his life Jesus had taught his disciples to make love the master-key of morals, by his death on Calvary he gave the word a still richer meaning. There, the apostles taught, on an April day in AD 30, and on a Roman cross, the supreme act of *agapē* had actually been performed in history – an act which made them all Christ's debtors and set them construing the word 'love' in terms of the cross on the hill. This is why the apostles find in the death of Christ a supreme incentive to Christian loving.

'As God's dear children,' says St Paul, who in I Cor. 13 had immortally set forth love's nature and necessity, 'live in love as Christ loved you and gave himself up on your behalf' (Eph. 5.1).

'In this is love,' wrote St John, 'not that we loved God but that he loved us and sent his Son to be the expiation for our sins. Beloved, if God so loved us, we also ought to love one another' (I John 4.10f.).

'Knowing that you were ransomed ... with the precious blood of Christ,' said St Peter, 'love one another earnestly from the heart' (I Peter 1.18-22).

Thus the apostles came to interpret the word love by the sacrifice of Christ, so that henceforth *agapē* became dyed with the crimson of Calvary and lit up with the light of the first Easter day. The word 'love', it has been said, always needs a dictionary. For Christians, that dictionary is Christ crucified and risen, and God's love made manifest in him.

'Love, and what you will, do,' wrote St Augustine in words often quoted. In terms of the New Testament, they might be amended to read, 'Love as the cross creates love, and do what you will.'

III

Concerning this 'sacrificial' love the apostles say three things.

The first is the point we have just made. St John sums it up: 'We love, because he first loved us.' (I John 4.19). Christian love, or *agapē*, is, or ought to be, our response to the divine love which gave us Christ as a sacrifice for our sins. It is the answering echo evoked in our hearts by God's love, and we are to show our gratitude by caring for our fellow men.

In the second place, such love is the fulfilment of the moral law as we have it in the Ten Commandments. 'He who loves his neighbour,' Paul explains, 'has fulfilled the Law' (Rom. 13.8). Why does the 'eleventh commandment' fulfil the first ten? Simply because every one who obeys it – who really cares for his neighbour – will never dream of murdering him, taking his wife, stealing from him, giving false evidence against him, or coveting his possessions.

Third – and most importantly – the eleventh commandment ought to be the law of the Christian's every-day living – not simply something to be talked about, but something to be done, and done by us. 'Let us put our love not into words but into deeds,' says the apostle, 'and make it *real*' (I John 3.18, Moffatt).

'Love never fails,' Paul assures us (I Cor. 13.8). By this he means that only love 'lasts on' into the next world, because love is the life of heaven. Yet, since it is also the law of the Christian's every-day living on earth, we do not misinterpret Paul if we stretch his words to mean that, however hard the road before us, love will always find a way. Love is always relevant, Reinhold Niebuhr has said, but 'never a simple possibility'. How to apply Christian love in social action, e.g., in industrial relations, today will pose many problems. Sometimes, too, its application will call for great firmness, even a being cruel in order to be kind, like Abraham Lincoln's when, seeing the horrors of the slave-market for the first time, he vowed, 'If ever I get a chance to hit this thing, I will hit it hard.' Yet, whatever the circumstances, such Christian action will always have about it that characteristic quality of 'caring', or *agapē*, which, we believe, is the very nature of God (I John 4.8) and was once for all shown in the gift of his Son for a world's saving (John 3.16).

15

The Unfamiliar Sayings
of Jesus

I

No prophet is acceptable in his own country,
Neither does a doctor work cures on his own acquaintances.

The first half of this saying of Jesus, found fifty years ago
in the sands of Egypt, we recognize at once; but the other
half is unfamiliar, undeniably apt, and possibly genuine.
With its combination of new and old (Mark 6.4f.) the saying
may fitly introduce this essay on 'The Unfamiliar Sayings
of Jesus'. Scholars know them as the *Agrapha* (literally 'un-
written things'), the term covering all sayings of Jesus not
found in the canonical gospels which have come down to
us from other sources.

What are these sources?

The first is the New Testament itself. As we shall see, St
Paul quotes one saying of Jesus not found in the four gospels
and echoes another. We can recover one more from an old
manuscript of Luke's gospel. And the apocryphal *Gospel
according to the Hebrews*, a lost variant of Matthew, now
extant in only a few fragments, contains two or three more.

The second source is represented by early Christian
writers. Sayings of Jesus not found in the canonical gospels
were sometimes quoted by early church Fathers like Justin
Martyr, who taught in Rome, and Origen and Clement of
Alexandria.

The third source is the sands of Egypt. Everybody has
heard of the papyri, those ancient documents written on
papyrus which modern scholars have disinterred from the

rubbish heaps of old Egypt where they have suffered sand-burial for two thousand years. Among many such documents there came to light, between 1897 and 1935, five fragments containing sayings of Jesus.

Finally, the Mohammedans, who regard our Lord as a prophet second only to Mahomet, preserve about fifty sayings of Jesus in their literature. We cannot be sure that any of them is genuine, but two are worth quoting:

> As Jesus walked one day with his disciples, they passed the carcass of a dead dog. The apostles said, 'How foul is the smell of this dog!' But Jesus said, 'How white are his teeth!'

The other is an inscription found on the wall of a mosque near Delhi:

> Jesus on whom be peace, has said: 'This world is a bridge. Pass over it. But do not build your dwelling there.'

This might be a genuine 'word of the Lord' – compare his parable of the Rich Fool (Luke 12.16-21) – but who can say for certain?

So let us take up the question of the genuineness of these uncanonical sayings ascribed to Jesus. Their total, if we include the Mohammedan ones, exceeds a hundred. How do we decide whether a saying is genuine or not? In many cases a decision is tolerably easy. The saying in question may flatly contradict what we know of Jesus from the canonical gospels – may be completely 'out of character'. For an example: our gospels, and especially Luke, are at pains to emphasize the special place our Lord had in his heart for women. When therefore we find some Egyptian Christians who favoured celibacy crediting Christ with the dictum, 'I came to destroy the works of the female', we need not hesitate to pronounce it false.

Other people wrongly attributed to Jesus something said by a prophet or psalmist; whilst other sayings are so clearly grotesque that no sensible man would believe that Jesus ever said them. Thus, some early Christians make him say, 'My mother, the Holy Spirit, took me and carried me by one of my hairs unto the great mountain Tabor.' Need we say more?

Roughly speaking, we have two tests for deciding whether a saying is true or false:

(1) *External evidence.* We must be sure that the source which preserves the saying is early and reliable; and of course if several such sources agree, we may be very sure.

(2) *Internal evidence.* The saying in question must agree in style and content with what we know of the mind of Jesus from our canonical gospels. If it does not, we do well to be suspicious.

Using these criteria, a succession of scholars from Albert Resch to Joachim Jeremias have gathered and sifted all these 'possible' sayings of Jesus. The result is to leave us with twelve to twenty which seem to pass all tests with flying colours and may be regarded as genuine. It is a small total, but some of the sayings are very vivid and valuable.

Let us start with three *stories* about Jesus.

(1) In Codex Bezae, one of our oldest gospel manuscripts, at Luke 6.5 a scribe has inserted a story about Jesus after the narrative about the plucking of corn on the sabbath:

> On the same day seeing a man working on the sabbath, Jesus said to him: 'O man, if thou knowest what thou doest, blessed art thou. But if thou knowest not, thou art accursed and a transgressor of the Law.'

Though it is no part of the gospel of St Luke, this little story rings true, both in style and content. We know how strictly the Scribes and Pharisees kept the sabbath. On that day you weren't allowed to fry an egg or walk more than half a mile. And yet Jesus seemed almost to go out of his way to heal sick people on the sabbath. Was his simply a humanitarian concern to insist that man is greater than any institution? This may be partly true, but it fails to explain the words with which Jesus wound up the cornfields controversy: 'So the Son of man is lord also of the sabbath.'

The sabbath-keeping enjoined in the Law was regarded as a foretaste of the true sabbath, i.e., the Messianic Age. The Law sabbath was the shadow; the kingdom of God, or Messianic Age, when it came, was to be the reality. (Hebrews makes much of this idea.) If this is the right clue, the reason why Jesus' apparently cavalier treatment of the sabbath so enraged the Scribes and Pharisees was that it carried the claim that the Messianic Age had begun and that he, as Messiah, was Lord of the sabbath. (Cf. John 5.10-18 which contains a like majestic claim by Jesus.)

Now come back to our story about the man working on the sabbath. Jesus accosts him: 'If you are doing what you are doing because you know that the time of the law and prophets is over and the kingdom of God is dawning (which is what, according to Luke 16.16, he did say) you are blessed. But if not, then your working on the sabbath is sheer impudence, as your law-breaking deserves to be condemned.'

This is a genuine *Agraphon*, and we do well to be thankful to the nameless scribe who preserved it.

(2) Irishly enough, the next unfamiliar story is very familiar. Yet the tale of the Woman taken in Adultery (John 7.53-8.11), though it now stands in the canonical gospels, belongs to the *Agrapha*. Since we have already discussed it in an earlier essay (on 'the Magnanimity of Christ' above p. 46), we do not dwell on it here. Enough to say that, though the story is no true part of St John's gospel, it has all the marks of authenticity.

(3) Our third story was found in a little parchment-book which an Egyptian woman had hung round her child's neck as a charm against evil spirits. It tells how Jesus encountered a chief priest in the Inner Court of the Temple:

> Jesus took the disciples into the place of purity itself and walked in the Temple area. A Pharisee named Levi, who was a chief priest, met them and said: 'Who has given you leave to walk in this place of purity and inspect these holy vessels without first bathing yourself and even without your disciples washing their feet?'
>
> At once the Saviour stopped with his disciples and replied: 'You are here in the Temple? Are you clean?'
>
> He answered: 'Yes, I am clean. I have bathed myself in the pool of David. I went down into it by the one stair and I came up by the other, and only when I had put on clean clothes did I come up here to look at these holy vessels.'
>
> The Saviour said to him: 'Alas for the blind that see not! You have washed yourself in flowing water in which dogs and swine lie night and day, and scoured your outer skin just as harlots and flute-girls do theirs, anointing and beautifying themselves to arouse men's desire, though inwardly they are full of scorpions and all evil. But my disciples and I, who according to you, have not bathed, have bathed ourselves in the living waters from above.'

Levi complains that Jesus and his disciples have broken the Temple rules by not washing themselves before entering the Inner Court. Now, Jesus was not being irreverent. The rule that a clean person should take a bath before entering the Inner Court was a rabbinical regulation, without basis in the Law, which Jesus rejected – see Mark 7.1-13. To Jesus' question, 'Are you clean?' Levi answers, 'Yes, I have bathed in David's pool and put on clean clothes.' 'Do you call this purity?' replies Jesus, 'The foulest men may lie night and day in such water and be not one whit cleaner. You, Levi, have cleansed only your body. Even loose women do this in pursuit of their business. But my disciples and I have bathed in God's living water.' (Cf. John 4.10-14 where Jesus speaks of 'living water' which is God's gift.) Jesus is making the same point as he made in Mark 7. In God's sight the only possible defilement is inward, as the only real purity is that of those whose hearts have been cleansed by God's grace.

There is no reason why this *Agraphon* should not be judged substantially genuine. It reflects 'the mind of Christ'.

II

Now let us turn to something different. Four of our genuine *Agrapha* concern discipleship. One of them is preserved by Tertullian who tells us it was spoken on the way to Gethsemane:

> No man can gain the kingdom of heaven who has not passed through temptation.

More memorable is the next saying on the cost of discipleship. We recall how often in the canonical gospels Jesus bade prospective disciples count well the cost. So it is in this unfamiliar saying preserved by Origen:

> He that is near me is near the fire
> And he that is far from me is far from the kingdom.

Someone had offered to follow Jesus. Have you considered what you are doing? he asks. To be near to me is to be near fire (cf. Luke 12.49) – the fire of tribulation and suffering. In other words, it is dangerous to be with Jesus – you may end up on a martyr's pyre. Would you then turn back, as the rich young ruler did? Ah then, says Jesus, you would miss the kingdom of God. The fire is only a way – a way through to the glory of God.

Yet, though Jesus can be stern with potential followers, he can also cheer his men with words of hope and confidence

as in this saying, found at Oxyrhynchus in Egypt, which
begins familiarly:

> For he who is not against you is for you

and goes on *un*familiarly:

> He that stands far off today will tomorrow be with you.

The saying shows our Lord's unbounded confidence in God's
power to turn foes into friends. The opponents of today may
be the followers of tomorrow. Not many years later it was
to find remarkable fulfilment when Christ's most intransigent
foe became his most intrepid apostle. (Before his conversion
Paul had gone about saying, 'God made Jesus a curse'. After
his conversion he went on saying it, but now he added two
words which made all the difference, 'for us'.)

The last unfamiliar saying addressed to disciples is quoted
so often in early Christian writings that its genuineness is
beyond dispute:

> Show yourselves tried (*dokimoi*) moneychangers

or, in its fuller form preserved by Clement of Alexandria:

> Show yourselves tried moneychangers,
> rejecting much, but retaining the good (*to de kalon katechontes*)

a saying clearly echoed by St Paul in I Thess. 5.21f.:

> Test (*dokimazete*) all things:
> Retain the good (*to kalon katechete*)
> And abstain from all bad coinage (*eidous*).

As always, Jesus goes to real life for his illustration. When
one of the money changers who did business in Jerusalem
at Passover time, was not sure of a coin offered him by a
pilgrim, he would let it fall on his glass-covered table, and
the sound it made would tell him whether it was good or
bad money. This is the background of our saying in which
Jesus warns his disciples against false teaching. 'Don't be
deceived,' he says, 'learn from the moneychangers, and
acquire a sharp ear for all that is false.'

The saying is still relevant. There are still men who debase
the coinage of Christ's realm and peddle counterfeit gospels
among the unwary – Christian 'deviationists' like Jehovah's
Witnesses or *avant-garde* Christian prophets who offer their
hearers emasculated versions of the historic gospel – 'half

Gospels', as **P. T.** Forsyth called them, 'with no dignity and
no future' for 'like the famous mule they have neither pride
of ancestry nor hope of posterity'. We have still a Christian
duty to test and try their pretensions and, where necessary,
expose them for the shams they are.

III

Two unfamiliar sayings concern the providence of God and
our faith in him. The first, found at Oxyrhynchus, says quite
simply:

> He himself will give you raiment.

It is reminiscent of the great passage on 'trust and tran-
quillity' in the Sermon on the Mount – the most 'Franciscan'
passage in the gospels, in which Jesus, pointing his disciples
to the birds of the air and the lilies of the field, says 'Shall
he not much more clothe you, O ye of little faith' (Matt.
6.25-34).

Our saying is of the same tenor. Jesus, we may suppose, is
sending out his men on a mission. He forbids them to carry
money. But will they not starve and have nothing to clothe
themselves with? 'O you little-faiths,' says Jesus, 'haven't
you a Heavenly Father? Can't you trust him? He himself
will provide your raiment.'

The other saying, which deals with prayer, is preserved
by Clement of Alexandria, and by Origen whose version is
fuller:

> Ask for the big things
> And the little shall be added to you:
> Ask for the heavenly things
> And the earthly shall be added to you.

When you pray, says Jesus, put first things first: God's
kingdom, not your own concerns. If you do this, you may
rely on him to remember your needs. The perfect illustration
is of course the Lord's Prayer where we are bidden first to
pray for the hallowing of God's name, the coming of his
reign, and the doing of his will; and only when we have done
this, are we encouraged to ask for provision (our daily bread),
for pardon (forgive us our debts) and for protection (deliver
us from evil).

IV

Every student of the gospels knows that Jesus gave his disciples a design for living in the kingdom of God, of which the Sermon on the Mount (Matt. 5-7) provides a summary. In this design the most distinctive thing is the law of love, or *agapē*, which Jesus made the master-key of morals. One of the most beautiful expressions of it is to be found in a saying which, according to Jerome, stood in the lost *Gospel according to the Hebrews*:

> Never be joyful
> Except when you look upon your brother with love.

'Brother' here means fellow-countryman, not fellow-disciple. So long as Christ's follower cherishes hateful thoughts about somebody he knows, he has no right to be glad. A true disciple is happy only when every barrier of bad feeling between himself and the other man is down.

Alongside this saying we may set the other one which St Paul quoted to the Ephesian elders at Miletus (Acts 20.35):

> Remember the words of the Lord Jesus, how he said 'It is more blessed to give than to receive'.

If the Greek word for *than* has an exclusive force here, as it has in Luke 18.14 ('This man, not the other, went home acquitted of his sins') the true translation here will be: 'Giving is blessed, not receiving'. In any case, for Jesus' friends the rule of life must be the conquest of selfishness. And is this not just another way of saying *agapē*?

Two more sayings – one about judgment, the other about work – may bring our little *florilegium* to a close. The first we owe to Justin Martyr. 'Wherefore also,' he writes, 'our Lord Jesus Christ said:

> In whatsoever things I find you, in these will I also judge you.

Our Lord is looking away to the great day. When he comes in glory, he will not go peering into the past; he will take men and judge them, as he finds them. And blessed are those, as Paul would say, whom he will find abounding in the work of the Lord.

The other saying, which was found at Oxyrhynchus and

reads like a saying of the glorified Christ, deals with work and worship:

> Wherever there are two, they are not without God:
> And where there is one only, I say I am with him.
> Raise the stone, and thou wilt find me:
> Cleave the wood, and there am I.

Notice the two kinds of work mentioned. Lifting stones and splitting wood may sound like the dreariest kind of labour, and the least spiritual. No, says Jesus, even such labour may be transfigured by a hidden glory. As in Matt. 18.20 he promises his presence to the two or three who gather in his name, so here he assures it to the humble toiler who believes in him. What seems like cheerless drudgery may be lustred by the unseen presence of the saviour.

On that note let us close. The unfamiliar sayings are not many, which is perhaps proof that the evangelists did their work so well that only stray bits were left here and there for later gleaners. Yet, few as they are, they are interesting and vivid, and not seldom memorable and challenging. They do but underline the impression which the canonical gospels make on any candid reader that no one ever spoke like this man.

16

Mission in the New Testament

As the word 'mission' comes from the Latin *mittere* 'send', so the word 'apostle' is from the Greek *apostellein* which likewise means 'send'. 'Mission' therefore means 'sending', and an 'apostle' is 'one sent' – a messenger specially authorized to act and speak for his sender.

When we talk about 'the apostles' we generally mean the twelve men Jesus called to proclaim his 'good news', and to form the nucleus of the new people of God, which is the church of Christ. But *the* apostle in the New Testament is not one of the twelve, neither is it Paul; it is their common Lord. No fewer than forty-four times in John's gospel is Jesus called 'the Sent-of-God', i.e., God's apostle. The writer to the Hebrews describes him as 'the apostle of our confession' (Heb. 3.1), that is, the one we acknowledge as sent by God.

All this takes us back to Jesus' own self-awareness. What this was, he hints at in the parable of the Wicked Tenants (Mark 12.1-9). The climax of the story comes with the words, 'He (the owner of the vineyard, God) had now only one (messenger) left to send, his own dear son. In the end he sent him.' In Christ God was his own apostle.

Any study of New Testament mission must start from the story of how God sent his Son as his apostle. The mission of the men we call 'apostles' has its source in the sending of Jesus by God.

I   The Mission of God's Apostle

Let us begin with two questions: What did Jesus, God's

apostle, proclaim? And what was the purpose of his mission? The answer to the first question is that Jesus came proclaiming the dawning of the kingdom of God (Mark 1.15). Now in the gospels this means the kingly rule or reign of God, and it is nothing if not divine and dynamic. It does not mean some man-made Utopia, still less some Communist's earthly paradise. It means a 'break-through' from the unseen world which lies ever over and around us. It means God in his royal power, and in fulfilment of his promises, invading history in order to deliver his people from their sins and woes, and the new order of things thus established.

It is in the mission of Jesus that God does this; for it is the very heart of the gospel that this dynamic rule of God really began when he sent his Son by his life, death and resurrection, to reconcile a sinful world to himself (II Cor. 5.19).

All began with Jesus' proclamation to his countrymen that this great reign of God, for which they had so long hoped and prayed, was now 'upon them'. Familiarity has dulled our ears to the wonder of it. What Jesus meant was something like this, 'The blessed time which Isaiah prophesied (52.7) has come. The reign of God is now dawning. Turn back to God and believe the good tidings' (Mark 1.14f.).

But the rule of God does not operate in a vacuum. By its very nature it has a *sphere* of rule, implies a people of God living under that rule – that is, a new society, a new Israel. So we have the answer to our second question. The purpose of Jesus' mission was to create a new people of God who would be what old Israel had failed to be – 'a light for revelation to the Gentiles' (Isa. 42.6) and so bring the saving knowledge of the only true God to all men. To this end Jesus called various men to follow him, their task being, in his own vivid metaphor, to 'hook' men for God.

Thereafter Jesus went through Galilee, first in the synagogues and later by the lakeside, proclaiming (mostly in parables) that God's great hour had struck and bidding men 'turn back' to God.

His next act (Mark 3.13ff.) was from among his growing body of followers to *appoint twelve men* that 'they might be with him' to learn the ways of God's kingdom, before being sent out as its messengers. Twelve had been the number of the tribes in old Israel. By choosing twelve men Jesus symbolically declared his purpose of creating a new people of God.

Their training over, Jesus sent his men forth, two by two, to proclaim the dawning kingdom and to gather God's people. Disciples (learners) had become apostles (special messengers). 'He who receives you receives me,' said Jesus, sending them out, 'and he who receives me receives him who sent me' (Matt. 10.40). Through Jesus, the twelve were emissaries of the Almighty himself.

Yet, though the mission was no failure (see Luke 10.17ff.), near at hand for Jesus lay deep disappointment. For when his Galilean ministry culminated in that great open-air meal we call 'the Feeding of the Five Thousand' (Mark 6.30-44), the crowds showed they were not minded to 'turn back' to God. Instead, in the event they saw the chance of a nationalist uprising against hated Rome, with Jesus as its leader (John 6.15). Not such was God's purpose for his people or for his apostolic Son. So, refusing to play the role they had cast for him, Jesus retired with his twelve men outside of Galilee, there in communion with his Father to rethink the strategy of the kingdom. By the time the little band reached Caesarea Philippi on their way back, God's will had become clear to him. If he was the Messiah, as Peter now confessed him to be, God willed that he should go to his triumph not by leading a revolt against Rome but by giving his life (like the Suffering Servant, Isa. 53) as a 'ransom for many' (Mark 10.45). Only so could God's reign come 'with power' (Mark 9.1) and the holy 'fire' be set blazing in the world (Luke 12.49).

So, marching on Jerusalem, Jesus made there his last appeal to old Israel. What happened is history. Israel made fatal refusal of its Messiah, failed to see its real vocation and destiny in him. Their Messiah 'had come to his own home, and his own people had received him not' (John 1.11).

Yet God's purpose was not to be defeated by the blind obduracy of his own people. If, like the contemptuous guests in the tale of the Great Supper (Luke 14.15-24), they spurned God's invitation, he would yet fill his house with folk 'from the highways and the hedges', and 'many would come from east and west to sit down at table' with the patriarchs in his kingdom (Matt. 8.11).

But, before this could be, the planted seed of the kingdom must be watered by the bloody sweat of his Passion, and from, and through, his death as the Servant Messiah would arise a new people of God, united not by the blood of Abraham but of Christ, to realize and fulfil the high vocation which old Israel had renounced. In that faith Jesus embraced the cross, as of his Father's appointing, in the conviction that by his representative sacrifice – and his triumph over death – the kingdom of God, set up 'with power', would be 'opened to all believers'.

II   The Apostolic Mission

The tremendous sequel to the cross we all know. God raised his Son from the dead, thus setting his seal on the sacrifice of the cross. If on the first Good Friday Caiaphas, Pilate and the rest thought that, by crucifying Jesus, they had stopped his mission, they were mightily mistaken. They had killed him, but destroyed him they had not. On the contrary, his mission went on, went victoriously forward, under his living leadership.

So we turn to what happened seven weeks later, on the Day of Pentecost (Acts 2).

If Jesus' appointment of the twelve had been the birthday of the church, Pentecost was its coming of age. On that day Jesus' followers, led by Peter, became vividly aware of a new access of divine power – the promised Holy Spirit – to equip them for their mission. Calling on his hearers to repent and be baptized in the name of Christ, Peter said: 'The promise is to you and to your children and to all that are far off, everyone whom the Lord our God calls to him' (Acts 2.38f.). The mission of the new Israel to the world had been inaugurated 'with power from on high' (Luke 24.49).

Soon the little church had grown to five thousand (Acts 4.4). The task before them was two-fold: (*a*) empowered by the Holy Spirit to 'speak the word of God' – the message of Christ's 'finished work' – with all boldness; and (*b*) in the name of the risen Lord to heal and do mighty works (Acts 4.29f.). They were not only to win converts among God's ancient people but also to gather in his scattered children, that there might be 'one flock, one shepherd' (John 10.16).

Among those earliest Christians the man who saw clearest

the wider outreach of the church was the first martyr Stephen. But he was not alone: in Acts 1-8 Luke shows how, in one way or another, Christ's envoys like Philip moved outwards beyond the bounds of Israel. With chapter 9 there steps on to the stage of history that 'envoy extraordinary' who, under God, did more than any other to spread the gospel in the world.

So large a place has Paul in the New Testament that we tend to think of him as the only apostle to the wider world. This is unfair to many others who also contributed notably to the wider propagation of the gospel – to St Peter and St John and many others whose names are now known only to God. Yet Paul's claim 'In my labours I have outdone them all' (I Cor. 15.10) is the merest truth. In three great journeys he planted little outposts of the church from Asia Minor in the east to Jugoslavia in the west, and fulfilled his ambition of preaching the gospel (though in chains) in the capital of the world. It is an almost incredible achievement.

How did Paul conceive of the range, the agency, and the goal of Christian mission?

First, the gospel was meant for *all men*, Greek and non-Greek, because all men were alike sinners standing in need of God's grace (Rom. 1.18-3.31). For the gospel, as he said, was God's saving power for everyone ready to take him at his living and delivering word in Christ.

Second, God means the church to be his *corporate missionary* to the world. God's plan, he says in Ephesians, is to unite all things in Christ (Eph. 1.9f.), and to this end his appointed agent is the church. Drawing its life from its risen and regnant head, the church is Christ's working Body designed to carry out God's purpose for men, as once Christ had done so in 'the days of his flesh'. In Christ God the Father wills universal community. In that nascent community 'the middle wall of partition' – the Law of Moses – has been broken down by Christ's cross, so that Gentiles 'once far off from grace and without hope and God in the world' have now become 'fellow citizens with God's people, members of God's household' (Eph. 2.19).

But, third – and here we glimpse the goal of Christian mission – this healing of an ancient division is but prelude to the movement, under God, of all creatures to ultimate unity in Christ. When that comes to pass, there will be a single new humanity enjoying access, through Christ his Son, to the 'one God and Father of us all', and forming a great living temple for 'a habitat of God in the Spirit' (Eph. 2.22).

Such is Paul's 'vision splendid' of the last end of Christian mission.

From Paul let us now turn to Peter, not to evaluate his own missionary achievement (though it was very significant), but to seize on something of importance which he says in his circular letter to the Christians in Asia Minor.

In I Peter 2.4-9 the apostle compares the church to a spiritual temple composed of living stones, cohering in and completed by Christ its living key-stone. This church, he says, has both a *priestly* and a *prophetic* function. Its priestly role is to offer up 'spiritual sacrifices' – prayers and praises plus acts of Christian love and service – for Christians, he declares, form 'a royal priesthood'.

Here, in germ, is the excellent doctrine on which Luther and the Reformers were to lay strong stress – the priesthood of all believers. Some have wrongly taken it to mean that the church has no priestly function (though according to Hebrews 10.19f. we are all *high* priests!). What it really means is that the priestly function of the church is something in which all members – and not merely the clergy – may share. What John Knox, for example, had in view was 'a corporate priesthood vested in the people'.[1] Every true Christian might be a priest, that is, someone worthy to stand before God, offer spiritual gifts, and pray for others. Yes, even a poor tenant farmer like William Burnes of whom his famous son wrote in 'The Cotter's Saturday Night' –

The priest-like father reads the sacred page.

(The epithet was well chosen; for there is extant a *Manual of Religious Belief* which that 'priest-like father' put together for the use of his family, resolved as he was to be a true priest in his own house.)

The church's *prophetic* role, according to St Peter, is 'to tell out the triumphs of him who called us out of darkness into his marvellous light'. If all believers may be priests, does not this mean that every sincere church member may be also an apostle? We may never stand up to preach, but day by day, by the way we live as by the service we render our fellow-men, we may be, in our small corner, ambassadors for Christ.

If St Peter has something to teach about 'the apostolate of the laity', the writer to the Hebrews (Apollos, or his spiritual twin brother) strikes another note which we need to hear. Not unjustly we may call it 'ecumenical'.

The letter to the Hebrews was addressed to some Jewish Christians in the Rome of Nero's day, who, threatened by state persecution, would fain have crept back under shelter of Judaism, a religion permitted by imperial Rome, as the new faith was not. Living too much in the Jewish part of their faith, they were remaining backwardly blind to the far horizons of their Christian calling. By contrast, the writer to the Hebrews was a man of the same bold, wide vision as the first martyr Stephen. He knew that Christ was the world's saviour and that his church was called to universal mission. So, again and again, in his letter he reminds his readers that Christianity is the final religion, and that, instead of shrinking back into Judaism, they must 'go forth to Jesus outside the camp' of Israel, and under his leadership embark on world mission (Heb. 13.13).[2]

Is not this a summons that we still need to hear? The church of Christ is not an ark of refuge to which the faithful may flee from the snares of the wicked world outside – shall we say, the world of 'the permissive society', industrial strife and thermo-nuclear bombs. The church becomes truly the church when, refusing to be merely Christ's 'mystical' Body, it becomes his working Body in the wider world. If we may bring this down to the congregational level, all our services in church should end with the idea not just that we are being sent *away*, but that we are being sent *out*, to live and practise our faith in the semi-pagan world around us. The church's Lord, Jesus Christ, our writer reminds us, 'is the same yesterday, today and for ever'. And the revelation we have in him is dynamic, is ever challenging us to new dimensions of Christian thought and action. Much land yet remains to be possessed in the name of Christ. We are called to go out and go forward in the steps of this unchanging but ever onward-moving Christ.

III The Warrant for Christian Mission

Why is mission an inescapable obligation laid upon the church of Christ?

Let us hear the answers of three modern Christian thinkers, one Swiss, one British, one American.

Why mission? Because, answers Karl Barth, the risen Christ has so commanded his followers. 'All authority in heaven and on earth has been given me. Go therefore and make disciples of all nations' (Matt. 28.18f.). The marching orders of him who holds, and will hold, all authority, envision the founding of the apostolic church; and because of Christ's abiding presence with his people, his summons to 'make disciples of all nations' is mandatory to the end of time.

Our second witness, P. T. Forsyth, finds his answer in the cross-cum-resurrection. By crucifying their Messiah, he says, old Israel rejected not only God's apostle but their own vocation in him. But there, in the cross, a universal divine kingdom was set up in history, and to the new Israel after Christ's triumph over death came the call to take the message of God's reconciling love to the world. We are saved into a church with a mission to the whole human race. 'It is not in our choice to spread the gospel or not' he concludes, 'It is our death if we do not.'[3]

Our third witness, Donald G. Miller goes to St Paul for his answer. 'It pleased God to reveal his Son to me,' wrote the apostle, 'that I might preach him to the Gentiles' (Gal. 1.16). In the high hour of his conversion God gave Paul to see Christ his Son victorious over death, but he gave him also a vision of a world waiting for him and in need of such a saviour. God's unique revelation of himself in Christ is our warrant for world mission. Man the sinner is alienated from God. The gospel of Christ crucified and risen is the divine answer to his need. Therefore the church must engage in mission.

All three answers might be summed up by saying that because we have seen the saving light of God's glory in Christ (II Cor. 4.6), we must share this redemptive revelation with all men.

IV Conclusion

Let us close this study of mission in the New Testament with three practical postscripts, the burden of all three being the need for us Christians to think 'biglier'.

(1) The cause of Christian missions today would gain greatly if we could get the mass of our church members to grasp the true – the biblical – meaning of the church, which is the people of God. It is so fatally easy for us to identify the church with a building – our own place of worship; or with a denomination, our own one of course; or even with a clerical class.

But the church is not a building, or a denomination, or a clerical class. It is the new and true people of God with an ancestry that goes back to Abraham, the father of the faithful, and a mission which in Christ embraces all men under the sun. If we could get Christian people thus to think 'bigly' about the church, our denominationalism would be seen in its proper proportions, and our eyes would be opened to the vision of 'the Coming Great Church' which is the ultimate aim of all Christian missionary endeavour.

(2) Though the church is the home of the Holy Spirit, which may be defined as 'God in action here and now', the Spirit's activity is not confined to the *institutional* church. Beyond that church's limits God's Spirit is at work in the wider world, moving in all sorts of men and situations creatively, cathartically, renewingly. (Of this fact the Charismatic Movement which is now, in one way or another, affecting all our churches, even the Church of Rome, ought to remind us. For the origins of Neo-Pentecostalism go back to a revival amongst North American negroes at the beginning of this century, and the avowed aim of the Neo-Pentecostalists is to defrost a frozen institutional church.) The realization of this truth should ever be urging us on to fresh conquests for Christ in the great non-Christian world today.

Not long ago, in a public lecture on 'the Holy Spirit the Comforter' Dr Michael Ramsey reminded his hearers of a scene in the famous Bayeux Tapestry (now in the cathedral of Caen). The tapestry tells in seventy-two pictures the story of the Norman Conquest – '1066 and all that'. In one scene

William the Conqueror is seen marching behind his troops with a drawn sword in his hand, evidently prodding them on. Beneath the picture are the words: 'King William comforteth his soldiers'. Not 'comforting' in the modern 'soft' sense of that word, but 'prodding' – inciting, urging on – is one of the Spirit's chief tasks today with us, the laggard soldiers of Christ, in a world that desperately needs the gospel.

(3) This brings us to the third *desideratum* for the church. As 'a deep theology is the best fuel for devotion', so a great gospel is the best incentive to Christian mission.

Why does the modern church not compel the respect of the nation, fire the devotion of youth, and rouse Christians to shape the world more and more according to God's will declared in Christ? Is it not because the gospel as we present it is not big enough to command conscience and tap the devotion which impels to mission? Our God is too small. We offer men a Christ who is too little to cope with world tragedy and sin wide as the human race. We crib, cabin and confine the work of the Holy Spirit, the Lord and Giver of life. Such reductionist versions of the apostolic gospel will never kindle to mission.

Only a gospel which takes seriously human sin and guilt, and has at its heart 'the Father of an infinite majesty', a commanding Christ and a redeeming cross – a gospel which, at the same time, proclaims these kingly apostolic truths in modern idiom and meaningful terms, is fit for the task of mission in such a world as ours. Proclaim such a gospel in ways that will come home livingly to modern man in his spiritual malaise and 'lostness', and the church will recover its note of authority, and people will not ask, 'Why mission?'. They will see it as the main article of a standing or falling church, and Christianity's quite ineluctable duty and its most glorious emprise.

NOTES

1. Gordon Donaldson, *The Scotsman*, 25 November 1972.

2. W. Manson, *The Epistle to the Hebrews*, Hodder & Stoughton 1951.

3. See *Revelation Old and New*, Independent Press 1962, ch. 3. On the whole subject consult G. H. Anderson (ed.) *The Theology of Christian Missions*, SCM Press 1962.

17

The Rock Apostle

Jesus called him a 'rock', but for centuries Peter has been a 'stone of stumbling' between Catholics and Protestants. Catholics hold that at his death Peter, as prince of the apostles and head of the church, bequeathed his role and powers to the head of the Church of Rome, and that the Pope's claim today to rule the universal church rests on the fact that he is the personal successor of St Peter. To this Protestants reply that no text of the apostolic age records this bequest by Peter of his special powers to the head of the Church of Rome, and that no bishop in the world, from the bishop of Rome down, can prove that he stands in such an apostolic succession. The true apostolic succession, they contend, is the *evangelical* one, the succession of those who proclaim the gospel of God's great grace in Christ, which was the good news preached by the first apostles.

What is the truth about Peter – the Peter of history? Let us begin with a 'potted biography' in the style of *Who's Who*, on the main facts of which most scholars would now agree, though some Protestants would still deny that Peter was ever in Rome:

Simon, alias Cephas (Greek, *Petros*). Born at Bethsaida. Father's name: Jonah (or John). Married and settled in Capernaum. Occupation: Galilean fisherman, along with brother Andrew. Gave up boat and business on being called by Jesus to become 'fisher of men'. Along with eleven others, appointed 'apostle' by Jesus, and took part in the mission of the twelve to the towns of Galilee, and was with him on the mount of Transfiguration. Present at the Last Supper in Jerusalem. First apostle to see the risen Christ who commissioned him to 'feed his sheep'.

Presided in Jerusalem on the Day of Pentecost, and acted as director of the young church for perhaps a dozen years. Later became leader of the Jewish-Christian mission, visiting Antioch, probably Corinth, and finally Rome. Martyred during the Neronian persecution, and buried in the Vatican area.

Publication: encyclical letter (with Silvanus) to Christians in Asia Minor.

Now let us fill in this outline and try to evaluate Peter as disciple, apostle and martyr.

I

Among Jesus' disciples Peter's primacy is indisputable. First to be called, his name always heads the list of the twelve. With the sons of Zebedee he belongs to that inner circle chosen to be with Jesus on certain high occasions. In dialogue with Jesus Peter regularly acts as the disciples' spokesman, as he has a way of taking the lead among them. Despite the special position of 'the beloved disciple' in St John's gospel, Peter's pre-eminence is still discernible (John 6.66f.; 13.36). At the Last Supper Jesus singles out Peter as the man best fitted to 'strengthen his brethren' after the crisis of Calvary (Luke 22.31f.). On the first Easter morning Jesus' message, to be conveyed by the women, is, 'Go and tell the disciples *and Peter*' (Mark 16.7).

But if Peter is courageous and forthright, he is also impetuous and volatile, with a weakness for saying the wrong thing on the wrong occasion, as at the Transfiguration or in Gethsemane ('Here are two swords' Luke 22.38). Clearly he was no plaster saint: when he was angry he could swear like a trooper; when his blood was up, he was ready, for his Master's sake, to do murder; and when he was cornered, he denied any personal knowledge of Jesus.

Why then did Jesus call him a 'rock' (Cēphas) and declare that 'on this rock' he would found his new people of God? Is it enough to say that this was the sovereign decision of Jesus and we must not question further? May we not say that, spite of his failings, Jesus saw in Peter the one 'born leader' among his disciples and the one fittest to rally them after the *debâcle* of the cross?

We turn now to the days after the resurrection which of course changed everything for the disciples – before it, like frightened sheep; after it, as bold as lions. The first to see the risen Lord (I Cor. 15.5; Luke 24.34), Peter was commissioned by Jesus to tend his 'little flock' – to feed, heed and lead them in the days to come (John 21.17). And this, according to Acts 1-12, he did. Until the early 'forties' Peter was unquestionably the dominant figure in the mother church.

Originally and inevitably, his work was in and around Jerusalem, after the happenings at Pentecost over which he presided. We find him healing, judging, and championing the faith before the Jewish authorities. When the gospel spreads to Samaria, he goes with John to lay hands on the new converts. But he makes real history when, at Caesarea, in response to divine guidance, he preaches to uncircumcised Gentiles and baptizes them. This bold action and his prominence in Jerusalem draw down on him the wrath of the Jews so that, to conciliate them, King Herod Agrippa has him arrested. After his release from prison, we are told (Acts 12.17) he went to 'another place' – not Rome, but 'underground', as 'wanted' men do nowadays. Possibly it was because of Herod's action that he now left the care of the Jerusalem church to James, the Lord's brother, whose conservative Christianity was less likely to arouse Jewish hostility. In so doing he was not abdicating the role given him by Christ. With James in charge of the local church, Peter now felt free to pursue his calling in fresh fields of action.

Peter's role now was to lead the Jewish-Christian mission, as Paul the Gentile Christian one. Present at the Apostolic Council of AD 49, over which James as head of the local church presided, Peter took Paul's line about the admission of the Gentiles to the church (Acts 15.7-11). But where did he go in the next decade? In Acts, Luke is so bent on following his hero Paul on the path to Rome that he says nothing about Peter. Yet from Paul (Gal. 2.11) we know that Peter went to Antioch, the cradle of Gentile Christianity – when, we cannot certainly say. It is also probable that he visited Corinth.[1] By AD 55 there was a 'Peter Party' in Corinth besides one owning allegiance to Paul and another to Apollos (I Cor. 1.12). Since these two latter owed their origin to the personal activity of Paul and Apollos in Corinth, we naturally assume that Peter had been there too.

Caesarea, Antioch and probably Corinth – but may we add Rome to the list of cities visited by Peter?

Nowhere does the New Testament say expressly that Peter went to Rome. The proof that he did is found by combining two pieces of New Testament evidence with the testimonies of Clement of Rome and Ignatius of Antioch.

It is commonly agreed that the two verses (John 21.18f.) about Peter's destiny in the last chapter of John's gospel indicate that, when they were written, Peter was known not only to be dead but to have died as a martyr. Next, in I Peter 5.13 we read: 'She (a church) who is at Babylon, likewise chosen, sends you greetings and so does Mark my son.' Here 'Babylon' is almost certainly (what it is in Revelation) a cryptic name for Rome. If so, Peter is writing, with the help of Silvanus, to the Christians of Asia Minor from the world's capital.

Near the end of the first century and at the beginning of the second we have two pieces of confirmatory evidence. Clement, bishop of Rome, in AD 96 writes to the Corinthians that Peter and Paul 'contended unto death' for the faith, and with them conjoins 'the great multitude among us' (i.e., in Rome) who likewise suffered. A dozen years later some words in a letter of Ignatius to the Christians in Rome suggest the like conclusion. To the same effect, later in the second century, speak Irenaeus, Tertullian and Dionysius of Corinth. Then, about AD 200, Gaius the Roman presbyter declares he can show the enquirer the 'trophies' (memorial monuments) of Peter and Paul on the Vatican Hill and the Ostian Way. It is uncertain whether these monuments marked the places of their burial or of their martyrdom. What is clear is that by AD 200 a monument to Peter stood on the Vatican Hill. On this site, a century later, the Emperor Constantine built a church. On it stands the present St Peter's.

Now pass down seventeen centuries. In AD 1950 Pope Pius XII startled the world by announcing that archaeologists had found Peter's grave beneath the Church of St Peter. He did not claim that they had identified the apostle's bones. What they had found was a ruined columnar monument. Does it mark the last resting-place of Peter's body? Or is it the 'trophy' mentioned by Gaius, and does it stand over the place not of his burial but of his martyrdom? We cannot certainly answer these questions. Peter *may* have been buried where the monument now stands; but the fact has not been demonstrated. What we may fairly claim is that there is adequate evidence that Peter did reach Rome and was martyred there.

II

We pass now to the famous words about Peter's place in the church (Matt. 16.17-19). No passage in the New Testament has so divided Catholic from Protestant. For Catholics it has long been the main scriptural proof-text for the doctrine of the papacy. Protestants have either declared it unauthentic or, accepting it as genuine, argue that the 'rock' on which Jesus will build his church is Peter's faith, not Peter's person.

Happily, in our time, both sides have modified their views. Now Catholics like Benoit concede that 'the universal authority of the Pope, founded on personal succession from St Peter, is in the end an object of faith for the Catholic.[2] On the other hand, Protestants like Cullmann take the passage to be a genuine saying of Jesus and agree that the rock is Peter's person.

Nor is it hard to argue its authenticity, Its poetic style (three tristichs, with four beats in each line), its Semitisms (the opening makarism, a word-play in Aramaic on Peter's name, 'gates of Hades' etc.) and its dominical imagery[3] ('rock' 'build' 'key') all point in this direction. What is really to be questioned is its *present setting* in Matthew's gospel. By inserting the passage here in his Markan framework, St Matthew has seriously obscured the original meaning of Peter's confession at Caesarea Philippi, where the point of the narrative lies chiefly in the announcement of suffering and Jesus' reprimand of Peter for thinking like a man and not as God. The most probable setting for the passage is after the Last Supper, on the eve of Christ's passion and of Peter's denial; for its tenor is the same as Jesus' words to Peter in the upper room: 'Simon, Simon, behold, Satan demanded to have you (plural), that he might sift you like wheat, but I have prayed for you (singular) that your faith may not fail; and when you have turned again, strengthen your brethren' (Luke 22.31f.).

If this view be accepted, let us consider the triple image in Jesus' promise to Peter.

'You are *Kepha* (Aramaic for 'rock'), and on this *Kepha* I will build my people of God (the Greek *ekklēsia* doubtless representing the Hebrew *qāhāl*).' The natural meaning is that Peter himself is the rock – the ground-rock on which

Jesus will found the new Israel, over which 'the gates of Hades' i.e., the powers of death, will not prevail.

'I will give you the keys of the kingdom of heaven.' In view of the biblical meaning of this image (cf. Isa. 22.22, 'I will lay the key of the house of David on his (Eliakim's) shoulder; what he opens no man shall shut, and what he shuts no man shall open') the 'keys' must signify the administration of God's household rather than merely refer to apostolic mission.

Finally, the power to 'bind' and 'loose' (rabbinical terms for 'forbid' and 'permit') surely means that Jesus is authorizing Peter to declare what is right and what is wrong in the new community to be built upon his person. Its base, or ground-rock, Peter will be, as he will exercise authority in it.

Nor did Peter disappoint Christ's confidence in his 'rock-man'. On the day of Pentecost he began to fulfil the promise of his name. For perhaps a dozen years he led, judged, and championed the young church in and around Jerusalem. Later he directed the Jewish-Christian mission, going certainly to Antioch and possibly to Corinth. In the early 'sixties' we find him (with John Mark) in Rome from which he counsels the Christians in Asia Minor, faced with persecution, to stand fast in the faith. And there is good reason to believe that, when his own time came, he was faithful unto death.

One thing more, and that of palmary importance, is to be said. In spite of Roman Catholic claims – and no appeal to 'tradition' will persuade the non-Catholic otherwise – Christ never authorized Peter to transmit his apostolic authority to his successors in Rome. As a matter of history, it was not until the third century AD that a bishop of Rome applied Matt. 16.17ff. to himself and his office. Moreover, modern studies of the office of the *shaliach* (which is Hebrew for 'apostle') in Judaism show that his authority was intransmissible. When the 'apostle' ceased to exercise it, it reverted to his principal, his sender. (See T. W. Manson, *The Church's Ministry*, 1948, chapter 2, for an excellent summary of the facts.) What our Lord had in mind in his promise to Peter was the upbuilding of the infant church after the resurrection, and the promise was unique and unrepeatable.

III

Where did Peter stand as a Christian?

A hundred years ago the critics of Tübingen averred that the early church was split down the middle between 'Petrinists' and 'Paulinists'. How many would maintain that thesis today? On the contrary, not a few would declare that in his Christian thinking Peter stood nearer Paul than any other apostle.

In I Cor. 15.1-11 we have Paul's word for it that on the basic facts of the gospel, or *kērygma*, they were at one. This agreement extended to their doctrine of salvation. When the two apostles clashed at Antioch over table-fellowship with Gentile converts, Paul said to Peter: 'We may be Jews by birth and not "Gentile sinners", but we know that a man is justified by faith, and not by doing what the Law demands' (Gal. 2.16). Despite his vacillation at Antioch, Peter's treatment of the Gentile Cornelius and his friends at Caesarea (Acts 10), his cordial recognition of Paul and Barnabas as apostles to the Gentiles (Gal. 2.1-10), and the lead which he gave at the Apostolic Council (Acts 15.7-11) show that on the question of Gentiles in the church Peter was *pro* Paul and against the 'Judaizers'.

Moreover, Peter and Paul were at one on the centrality of the cross in the doctrine of redemption. Both held that 'Christ died for our sins according to the scriptures'. This doctrine goes back of course to Christ himself, but it may well have been Peter who first pointed men back to Isa. 53 for light on the meaning of the cross. Twice in Peter's speeches in Acts and twice in prayers when he was present, Jesus is called 'the Servant of God' (*pais theou.* Acts 2.13, 16; 4.27, 30). This is surely no accident. When Jesus had first spoken about a suffering Messiah, Peter had recoiled in horror at the very idea (Mark 8.32). Yet it was to the man who had so reacted that the risen Lord had first shown himself alive (I Cor. 15.5). Is it not consonant with what we know of him that the man who had tried hardest to divert Jesus from the way of the cross should have made the great *volte face* and been the first to proclaim that the death of Jesus the Servant had been according to his Father's will and for the sins of the many? How important 'the Servant Christology' was to his thinking is shown in I Peter 2.21-25 where Isa. 53 is fully applied to Jesus.

IV

When we compare the two apostles, we should remember the advantages each had over the other. Peter's was *historical*. He had been a full-time disciple of Jesus in 'the days of his flesh', had lived through all the events which took him to the cross, had been the first to see him risen. By contrast, Paul had arrived comparatively late on the Christian scene, never having known Jesus during his earthly ministry. Paul's advantage over Peter was *intellectual*. Blessed with a powerful mind and trained in Gamaliel's school, he was far better fitted to think out all that the new faith meant than the ex-fisherman Peter whose gifts lay rather in action than in writing.

Yet Peter was at heart with Paul on the universal outreach of the church. May it not have been from Jesus himself that Peter first learned that with the coming of the kingdom of God the day of the Law's domination was over (Luke 16.16) and that many would come from east and west and sit down with the patriarchs in that kingdom (Matt. 8.11)? So we may explain why Peter baptized Cornelius and his friends without saying a word about circumcision and at Antioch broke the Jewish law by eating and drinking with Gentile converts (Gal. 2.12). What Peter did by Christian instinct at Caesarea and Antioch, it fell to Paul the trained thinker to work out to its theological conclusions. In Christ they were *par nobile fratrum*.

Our Lord did not err in naming Peter the rock and predicting that on him he would build his church. From the day of Pentecost in Jerusalem in AD 30 to the day in the mid sixties of the century when he died in Rome, he abundantly justified his Master's confidence in him. Though we cannot accept their belief that the Pope's universal authority is founded on personal succession from St Peter, Catholics are well warranted in calling him a prince among the apostles and setting his name beside that of Paul. To all Christians, whatever be their ecclesiastical label, he is a shining example of how a warm-hearted and enthusiastic, if sometimes unstable and volatile, man can be conquered by the love of

Christ, deepened by training in his school, disciplined by hardship, and used by God to spread the gospel in a ministry which was consummated with a martyr's crown.[4]

NOTES

1. As Dionysius, bishop of Corinth, testified in the second century.

2. P. Benoit, *Jesus and the Gospel*, Darton, Longman & Todd 1974, vol. II, p. 174.

3. Cf. Matt. 7.24-27; Luke 11.32; Matt. 23.13.

4. In this essay I have been deeply indebted to O. Cullmann's *Peter: Disciple, Apostle, Martyr*, SCM Press 1962; but I have profited from P. Benoit's admirable review of Cullmann in *Jesus and the Gospel*, vol. II, pp. 154-175.

18

Stephen the Trail-blazer

Acts 6.8-8.3

Stephen (which in Greek means 'crown') is a fit name for
the first man to wear the martyr's crown in that 'noble army'
which stretches from apostolic times to our own, and is
lustred by names from Ignatius to Dietrich Bonhoeffer. Yet
Stephen was, above all else, a spiritual trail-blazer; indeed
he became the proto-martyr precisely because, following his
Lord's light and leading, he blazed the trail for others to
follow in his train.

Bernard Shaw[1] once dismissed Stephen as 'a bore' who
inflicted on the Sanhedrin 'a tedious sketch of the history of
Israel'. Doubtless this is the first impression which a reading
of Stephen's apologia (Acts 7) makes on the ordinary reader.
But wrong reading it is. Thanks to modern scholars, Stephen's
true spiritual stature begins to glimmer through the mists
of antiquity. From them he emerges not merely as the first
Christian hero but as the man who, sensing the true import
of Christ's words and works, proved himself the precursor
of Paul, the writer to the Hebrews, and all who realized that
the good news of Jesus was meant for all men.

I

Temple and Torah – the 'Place' where God had chosen
to set his name and manifest his presence, and the Law of
Moses – God's revealed will for his people, epitomized in
the Ten Commandments – these were the twin bastions of
that Judaism which provided the religious background for
the historic ministry of Jesus. But, by the evidence of the
gospels, he had declared that the day of both was over: with
the dawning of the kingdom of God the era of 'the law and

the prophets' was at an end (Luke 16.16), the Temple's doom was writ (Mark 13.32; Luke 13.35), he himself was some sort of New Torah (Matt. 5.21-48), and the purpose of his ministry was to create a new Israel, a new people of God, in which the Gentiles would find a place (John 2.19; Mark 14.58; Mark 11.17; 12.9; Luke 13.29; John 4.21f.; 10.16).

Understandably, the revolutionary import of this teaching was slow to dawn on the first apostles with their 'kingdom-to-Israel' outlook (Acts 1.6) not yet transformed by the event of Pentecost. Stephen the Hellenist Christian it was who first grasped the true tenor of Christ's teaching about the ultimate outreach of the gospel, and paid for it with his life.

'This man,' said his accusers, 'is for ever saying things against this holy place and against the Law; for we have heard him say that this Jesus of Nazareth will destroy this place and alter the customs handed down to us by Moses' (Acts 6.13). Luke says their testimony was 'false'. Yet from Stephen's apologia before the Sanhedrin we may think it was not so much 'lying' as insidiously 'slanted' against him.

What is the gist and 'drift' of that 'tedious' speech? To be sure, Stephen does (as Shaw charges) re-tell the story of God's dealings with Israel from Abraham onwards. But how skilfully he does it in order to show how deaf to God's purpose and disobedient to his prompting the men of Israel had been!

Read your scriptures, says Stephen in effect, and you will see that the scriptures themselves bid you look beyond Temple and Torah. God has never been tied to the soil of the Holy Land, neither is the Temple needed for his dwelling with men. Every advance in Israel's history has involved the forsaking of the static, the local, the traditional. By his Holy Spirit, God has always been urging Israel to 'go out' and exchange the known for the unknown. All Israel's God-led deliverers – Abraham, Joseph, Moses – have been men who 'ventured upon vision' and abandoned home and kinsfolk in response to the call of God. Not the solid and static Temple but a portable tent of testimony has been the palladium of his true people; and it is Moses, foretelling a future prophet, and King David divinely debarred from building a temple, who are his pointers forward. Yet what have the men of Israel done? They have spurned the leading of God's Spirit, rejected their deliverers, persecuted God's prophets, and now, to crown all their sins, they have murdered God's righteous one, his Servant Messiah, Jesus.

Trenchant, not 'tedious', is the word for that speech which must preserve the gist of what Stephen said. No wonder his hearers were touched to the raw, ground their teeth with fury, and set about stoning the speaker.

Though he was cut short when he came to his climax, there is enough in Stephen's apologia to suggest that he had understood Jesus' teaching about the fate of old Israel and the mission of the new one destined to arise through his death and resurrection. Doubtless in those synagogue debates with his foes (was Paul among them?) he had argued that the work of Jesus meant the abrogation of the whole Temple order and its supersession by a new edifice 'not made with hands'. In a word, Stephen had, however dimly, perceived that Christianity spelt the end of Jewish privilege and the dawning of a new universal kingdom of God.

II

In Luke's account of Stephen's martyrdom we find three things worthy of note: first, his dying prayer for his executioners, 'Lord, do not hold this sin against them', so reminiscent of Christ's word from the cross (Luke 23.34); second, his words describing his vision of the glorified Christ, 'I see the Son of man standing at God's right hand'; and third, the historian's pregnant comment, 'And the witnesses laid down their coats at the feet of a young man named Saul'.

'If Stephen had not prayed,' said St Augustine, 'the church would not have had Paul.' Beyond doubt one factor in Paul's conversion was the fearless faith of the first martyr. Yet before this Paul must have known what Stephen stood for as a Christian. Not the least of the many debts which Paul owed to his Christian predecessors was that he owed to Stephen. He it was who blazed the trail for the man who, by the grace of God, did more than any other to spread the gospel in the world and turn the tides of history.

In his famous essay on Paul, Dean Inge describing his conversion on the Damascus Road,[2] puts it thus:

'The Spirit of Jesus', as he came to call it, spoke to his heart, and the form of Jesus flashed before his eyes. Stephen had been right; the Crucified was indeed the Lord from heaven. So Saul became a Christian; and *it was to the Christianity of Stephen, not to that of James the Lord's brother, that he was converted.*

Paul's own account of the event which cut his life in two we have in his letter to the Galatians: 'God was pleased to reveal his Son to me that I might proclaim him among the Gentiles' (Gal. 1.15f.). If in the high hour of his conversion Paul saw not only the living Christ but the vision of a waiting world, and of himself as God's *apostolos* – his special messenger – to it, was he not following in the steps of Stephen and taking up the torch from his dying hands?

For reasons of place (the Sanhedrin) and time (the early 'thirties' of the first century) we should not expect Stephen to employ 'missionary' language like this to his accusers. What we might expect on his lips are anticipations of the new Israel's call to world mission, and this, in germ, is what we take to be the import of his apologia. The day of Temple and Torah is over. The Holy Spirit is the Spirit of advance. To his true servants God is saying, 'Like Abraham leave the old home and the old ways and go out in faith wherever I lead you.'

There is one more small but important piece of evidence that Stephen had glimpsed the universal mission of the new Israel. As he stood before his enraged accusers, Stephen had a vision of the glory of God and Jesus standing at God's right hand. 'I see,' he is recorded to have said, 'the Son of man standing at God's right hand'. Here, in Acts 7.56, we have the only instance of that title on any lips but those of Jesus himself. Now, in Dan 7.13f., from which Jesus derived it, the destiny of 'one like a son of man' is exaltation to the very presence of the Almighty, and to him is given 'dominion and glory and a kingdom, that all peoples, nations and languages should serve him'. Does not Stephen's name for Jesus mean that he knew that his sovereignty was to embrace all nations without distinction? While his Jewish fellow-Christians still clung to the rites and customs of old Israel, Stephen saw that the glorified Christ was on the throne of the world, and that the role of the new Israel was to go out and onward under the Son of man's leading?

So Stephen paved the way for Paul.

III

But that is not yet the whole story. Early in the 'sixties' of the first century a church leader whom we know as the writer to the Hebrews – or, for short, *Auctor* – sent a noble letter to some Christians in Rome. Threatened with persecution as Christians, they were tending to shrink back under cover of Judaism, a religion permitted by Rome as Christianity was not. *Auctor* stood in the spiritual succession of Stephen and his letter carries further the argument which the proto-martyr had begun to develop in the 'thirties'.

As we have shown, Stephen had seen that what may be called 'the Jesus Movement' was something other and greater than Judaism, that the Temple and the Torah were outworn, and that God was calling his people to go out into the wider world under the leadership of the glorified Son of man.

When we turn to Hebrews, we find parallel after parallel between Stephen and *Auctor*. The latter's message is summed up in two verses from his final chapter: 'Therefore let us go forth to him (Jesus) outside the camp (of Israel), bearing abuse for him. For here we have no lasting city, but we seek the city which is to come (the heavenly Jerusalem)' (Heb. 13.13f.). Earlier he had given his readers reasons for embarking on this new and greater Exodus. First, the Law is antiquated. Unable to bring anything to perfection, it is superseded in Christianity which opens up a new and living way to God (Heb. 7.18f.; 10.20). Second, God's call to his people is now, as it was to Abraham long ago, 'Go out in faith' (Heb. 10.37f.; 11). Third, Christians are summoned to 'the eschatological life'. This high vocation for them Stephen had glimpsed when he had argued that God's revelation was not confined to Israel and the Holy Land and had named Jesus the Son of man to whom God had promised universal sovereignty. Now, some thirty years later, it finds fuller expression in *Auctor*'s sublime vision of the pilgrim church on its way to the heavenly Zion (Heb. 12.18-29), following in the steps of Jesus, its great *Archēgos*,[3] who for the joy set before him had endured the cross and had now taken his seat at the right hand of the Majesty on high.

NOTES

1. *Androcles and the Lion*, Constable 1929, p. lxxxv.

2. W. R. Inge, *Outspoken Essays* First Series 1919, p. 218, my italics.

3. The *Archēgos* (Heb. 2.10; 12.2), 'initiator' or 'pioneer', has been well likened to the strong swimmer who carries the rope ashore and so makes rescue for all who follow him.

The 'pioneers' in this new thinking about Stephen have been William Manson in his *Epistle to the Hebrews*, Hodder & Stoughton 1951, and C. F. D. Moule, in *The Birth of the New Testament*, A. & C. Black 1962, to both of whom I am indebted.

19

Apollos the Alexandrian

Acts 18.24-28; I Cor. 1-3

A strange episode this in Luke's record of the apostles' 'Road to Rome'. A modern journalist might describe it as 'the case of the evangelist with the defective gospel'. It is the tale of Apollos the Alexandrian Christian who, on reaching Ephesus after Paul had left the city for Antioch, learned the full truth of Christianity from Aquila and Priscilla, then crossed to Corinth and there, in public debate, trounced his Jewish adversaries.

Can we discover why Apollos, arguing the same point with the Jews, was so much more successful than Paul, by Luke's record (Acts 18.5f.), was, and why in his preaching at Corinth he drew after him a band of partisans who cried, 'Apollos – not Paul, not Peter – is the man for us!'?

Our first question is – What does Luke mean when he says that Apollos 'had been instructed in the way of the Lord'? (The Western text adds: 'in his own land' i.e., Alexandria. If this is the right reading here, the gospel had reached Alexandria, as it had reached Rome, before AD 50.) 'The way of the Lord' suggests the mode of life taught by Jesus to his followers – the ethics of the Sermon on the Mount. To this account of Jesus' moral teaching he added an accurate outline of 'the facts about Jesus' (Acts 18.25).

Though some people today might reckon these adequate qualifications for a preacher of the gospel, Aquila and Priscilla, quite rightly, did not, and promptly took him in hand. What serious gaps in his Christianity did they repair with such evident success? How did they turn his defective gospel into an effective one, as witness what happened when Apollos went on to Corinth?

His first defect was that 'he knew only the baptism of

John' (Acts 18.25). Of Christian baptism he had no proper
understanding. In spite of Christ's baptism on Calvary,
the resurrection and the Pentecostal gift of the Holy Spirit,
Apollos had got no further in his understanding of baptism
than those who had heard the Baptist on the banks of Jordan.
All he knew of it was a water-baptism which symbolized a
turning to God in penitence for past sins because the day of
the Lord was near. Of Christ's great baptism in blood (Mark
10.38; Luke 12.50) and of the sacrament deriving from it in
which men, baptized 'in the name of Christ', were incorpor-
ated in the new community of the crucified and living Lord
Jesus, so that they received forgiveness of their sins and the
gift of the Holy Spirit, Apollos evidently knew nothing.
Here Aquila and Priscilla could, and surely did, enlighten
his ignorance; and though Acts does not record that Apollos
submitted to Christian baptism, in view of Acts 19.1-7 we
may be tolerably sure that he did.

What further defect did Aquila and Priscilla discover in
Apollos's Christianity? You will find a clue to the answer
in Acts 18.28. When later, in Corinth, Apollos debated in
public so effectively with the Jews, the burden of his argument was that 'the Messiah is Jesus'. Clearly before his
meeting with Aquila and Priscilla, his Christianity had
been 'Messianism without the belief that the Messiah had
come'.[1] In other words, he had seen in Jesus the colleague
and successor to John the Baptist, a prophet calling Israel
to repent in view of the future coming of the kingdom of
God. (His modern counterpart would be Bultmann who
finds in Jesus a Messianic prophet calling men to decision
in view of an imminent kingdom of God. But Apollos would
seem to have been surer than Bultmann is of 'the facts about
Jesus'!) What Aquila and Priscilla taught Apollos was that
the kingdom had dawned and Jesus was the Messiah, that
in fact he was the kingdom.

A momentous advance indeed! Near the end of his life
Karl Barth, being asked if his view of the person of Christ
had changed over the years, answered, 'Yes, at first I thought
Jesus was the prophet of the kingdom. Now I know that he *is*
the kingdom.' What a mighty difference this discovery must
have made to the preaching of Apollos! For it is one thing
to believe that Jesus is simply the prophet of the kingdom,
quite another to believe that he is himself God amongst us

in his saving sovereignty (which is what the kingdom of God means in the gospels).

Here let us add two comments with reference to our contemporary Christianity.

We have still in our churches many whose Christianity is as defective as was that of Apollos before he met Aquila and Priscilla. They are ready to see in Jesus a supreme prophet, a truly inspired man of God, the best indeed that ever lived. But they boggle at the idea that he is 'God's presence and his very self' active in the affairs of men, God's saving purpose embodied in human flesh. Yet unless, as Paul, Priscilla and Aquila surely held, God was really in Christ, uniquely and decisively, we have no good news for a sin-sick world. If Jesus is not the kingdom of God incarnate – God manifest in the flesh – but only one more man, however good and great, we had better erase the word 'gospel' from our vocabulary. We are in no better case than the Unitarian preacher who came to win converts to his creed among the down-and-outs of Aberdeen. On the third night of his mission a fallen woman out of the crowd told him that he had better pack up and go home. 'Your rope', she explained, 'is not long enough for the likes of me.'

Our second comment is practical. How wisely Aquila and Priscilla acted when they found how defective was their friend's view of Christianity! Tempted they might well have been to stand up in synagogue and correct his errors. Instead, they privately took it in hand to teach him 'the truth as it is in Jesus'. What spiritual dividends that private counselling was to yield! Thanks to his two mentors, Apollos had now a real gospel to preach, so that when he moved on from Ephesus to Corinth, he showed himself not only a brilliant evangelist but by virtue of his expertise in the scriptures he became 'the patron saint of Christian evidence societies, the father of apologetics'.[2]

I Apollos in Corinth

Now, supplementing Acts 18.24-28 from I Cor. 1-3, let us follow Apollos west to Corinth.

It was probably late in AD 52 that Apollos began his mission in that large pagan city. There not only did he debate with the Jews but he tended the young shoots of Paul's planting:

'I planted, Apollos watered,' wrote Paul, 'and God made things grow' (I Cor. 3.6).

Yet the mission of Apollos had two very different results. (1) According to Acts 18.28, he showed himself a doughty debater, proving from the scriptures that the Messiah was Jesus. The verb Luke uses – *diakatelegchein* – is a strong one. It means that he 'floored' his opponents.

(2) Not so happy was the second effect. From I Cor. 1-3 we gather that, all undesignedly, the preaching of Apollos sparked off that foolish party-strife, reported by 'Chloe's people', which, among other things, moved Paul in AD 55 to write I Corinthians. Yet these two things – his success in debate with the Jews and the outbreak of party strife – may not have been so unconnected as might appear.

To explain this, we must consider what manner of man Apollos was. 'I think,' said 'Rabbi' Duncan, 'that he was an intellectual – a man after the type of Philo the Jew.'[3] This judgment probably contains much truth. Recall his origins. While Apollos was growing up in the ghettoes of Alexandria, the city's leading theological thinker was beyond any doubt Philo (20 BC – AD 50). What was his particular line of theological expertise?

Convinced that the monotheistic God of the Jews was the one God of the Greek philosophers, Philo pursued what he called 'the path of figurative interpretation (of the scriptures) so dear to philosophical souls'. So adept was he in allegorical exegesis of the Old Testament that he found in passage after passage of the Pentateuch the best wisdom of the Greeks – Stoic as well as Platonic. Thus he derived the three Greek cardinal virtues – prudence, courage and self-control – from the three rivers – Pishon, Gihon and Tigris – of Gen. 2, and he held that it was the Stoic Logos which spoke to Moses in the burning bush.

Whether Apollos ever actually heard Philo in Alexandria – and he may well have – it is likely that he took the same theological line as his distinguished co-religionist. Here we may find the reason why he succeeded in those debates with the Jews of Corinth. Master of allegorical exegesis, he was able to find in the Old Testament type after type of Jesus the Messiah.

On the other hand, when he preached, he knew well how to harness the wisdom of Hellas in the service of the gospel.

Such preaching was well calculated to charm Greeks who were quick to contrast it with the less stylish *kērygma* of Paul who kept hammering away at the cruciality of the cross (I Cor. 2.2). Thus arose that clique in the church at Corinth whose slogan was 'I am of Apollos', as doubtless it was in reaction to the Apollos faction that there arose the party of Paul, their first father-in-God (I Cor. 4.15). When this happened, is it surprising that yet others said, 'A plague on both your parties!' and lined themselves up under the banner of Peter, the leader among the original twelve apostles – more especially if, as is possible, Peter had in fact visited the church at Corinth?

If we are right, the whole trouble originated in the excesses of the Apollos party. It was they who led Paul to say such hard things about 'the wisdom of men' in I Cor. 1-3. One point, however, must be underscored. Never once in his letter does Paul disparage Apollos personally. On the contrary, he regards him as a true colleague (I Cor. 16.12), a fellow-agent with himself in the propagation of the gospel (I Cor. 3.5ff.): theirs, he says, had been good team-work for God. What grieved Paul was not his colleague Apollos but his partisans, those silly sciolists who so idolized the brilliant Alexandrian that they were wrecking the peace of the church. Such adulatory advocacy of a church leader and his gifts is not without parallel in later ecclesiastical history.

The nub of Paul's complaint against the Apollos faction was that they made of the gospel a philosophy, a wisdom, a *gnōsis*, when really it was a spiritual *power* reaching down with God's redeeming grace in Christ and his cross to the very moral foundations of life. ('To be sure,' Paul says, 'I have a secret wisdom also, but it is for mature Christians, not babes in Christ like you.' See I Cor. 2.6ff. and 3.1ff. By this Paul probably meant the wider implications of God's redemption of the race in Christ – his divine plan for the world, as he was to spell it out later in Ephesians.) For Paul, the gospel was first and foremost a *dynamis*, God's power, centred in the cross, which produced 'righteousness, sanctification and redemption' (I Cor. 1.30), that is, real forgiveness, a new life of holiness and deliverance from bondage to old evil ways. 'Jews demand signs,' he said, 'and Greeks seek wisdom, but we preach Christ crucified, a stumbling block to the Jews and folly to the Gentiles, but to those who are called, both Jews and Greeks, Christ the power of God and the wisdom of God' (I Cor. 1.21f.).

So the sum of Paul's counsel to the quarrelling Corinthians is this: 'An end to all these foolish factions, or you may have to answer to God for them! We apostles – Apollos, Peter and myself – are simply human agents in bringing you the gospel. Servants of Christ we are, fellow-labourers in God's service, as you are God's field or building on which we work. Therefore never, never make mere men a cause for pride and boasting!'

But, as is so often his way, Paul rounds off his warnings with a sentence which lifts us from the pettiness of their party-strife in Corinth up to the spiritual empyrean of God's purpose in Christ:

> For all things are yours, whether Paul or Apollos or Cephas, or the world or life or death, or the present or the future – all are yours, and you are Christ's, and Christ is God's (I Cor. 3.21f.).

To a church bedevilled by party-strife what a soaring and salutary recall to the greatness and the grandeur of the gospel! Does it not still speak to us with our ecclesiastical party – labels – 'I am of Knox', 'I am of Luther', 'I am of Wesley', 'I am of Peter the rock apostle' – and our all too parochial concepts of what Christianity is?

'All things are yours' Paul tells us as he did the Corinthians. The whole world-order – all men and times and circumstances – belongs to the Christian, and Christianity is a way to meet and master all that life holds. But how? What is the secret? The answer comes in the next four words: 'And you are Christ's'. When Paul says, 'You belong to Christ' this is not just a piece of pious blah. What he means is that the essential thing in Christianity is a personal relationship to Christ. So often we talk as if Christianity were simply a set of opinions about this or that current issue or problem, be it pacifism, pollution (moral and physical) or 'bishops in presbytery'. Of course on such issues the Christian is called to make up his mind and take his stand. But the paramount, the indispensable, thing in Christianity is a personal relationship to a living person and the conviction that he is the only true and living way to God.

Yet, having said this, Paul is not quite finished. With four further words he clinches the whole matter: 'And Christ is God's'. Christ is not simply some people's private hero, or the personal property of any religious sect or denomination. He is part of the last reality in the universe. The supreme truth about the carpenter is that he comes from the creator. And when we build on Christ, we are building not on any shifting quicksand but on the eternal granite which is God.

Thus petty party strifes can have their precious by-products if, as at Corinth, they can evoke such statements of the grandeur of the gospel.

II Apollos and Hebrews

Now, in the end, let us return to 'our brother Apollos' as Paul styles him (I Cor. 16.12).

Some people may wish that the New Testament had included a letter – or a sermon – from Apollos: some sample of the way in which he used the wisdom of Hellas in the service of the gospel. With this in our hands, how much better we might have appraised the apostle whom Paul accounted a true fellow-labourer in Christ's service!

And yet may not our regret at the lack of a letter from the pen of Apollos be misplaced?

Whose hand wrote the Epistle to the Hebrews – that religious masterpiece which portrays Christ as the perfect priest who by his self-sacrifice on the cross has opened up for us a new and living way into the presence of God; which contends that Christianity is the fulfilment of all that the ritual of Jewish Law – the whole system of priest and sanctuary and sacrifice – could only foreshadow; which in passage after passage calls on its readers (probably in Rome) to go forth into the world with the gospel under the leadership of the living and unchanging Christ?

It was not Paul's hand. On this modern scholars agree. Yet it is the work of a man belonging to Paul's circle (see Heb. 13.23 'I have news for you: our friend Timothy has been released!'). Why should it not have been Apollos, as Luther and many modern scholars have surmised? Go back to Luke's pen-portrait of Apollos in Acts 18 from which we started. There Luke tells us four things about Apollos:

(1) He was a Jewish Christian.
(2) He was an eloquent preacher.
(3) He was a native of Alexandria.

(4) He was a *maestro* with the scriptures.

All these things fit Apollos like a glove. Without doubt the nameless author of Hebrews was a Jewish Christian. His highly rhetorical style plus his habit of stopping to exhort his readers proclaim the practised preacher. He interprets Christianity in terms of the two-storeyed view of reality – the shadowy and the real – as Alexandrians like Philo did (see especially Heb. 8.5; 9.23ff.; 10.1), which goes back to Plato. And he allegorizes the scriptures – witness what he does with Melchizedek in chapter 7 – to show that Christ and his salvation are the fulfilment of the types and cultus of Judaism.

We cannot prove that Apollos wrote Hebrews. But if it was not the brilliant Alexandrian, it must have been, spiritually speaking, the twin brother of the man with the defective gospel whom Aquila and Priscilla befriended and taught the full truth about Christ and the kingdom.

NOTES

1. Johannes Weiss, *History of Primitive Christianity*, 1937, vol. I, p. 317.

2. T. W. Manson, *Studies in the Gospels and Epistles*, Manchester University Press 1962, p. 257.

3. J. Duncan, *Colloquia Peripatetica*, p. 59.

20

The Areopagitica
Acts 17.22-31

Nowadays let the freedom of what Burke called 'the Fourth Estate' be threatened, and the odds are that some pressman will quote (as it were Holy Writ) John Milton's pamphlet on the theme, the *Areopagitica*. The title really belongs to the speech Paul is said to have made to the Court of the Areopagus in Athens. Few passages in Acts have excited more scholarly debate than Luke's account of Paul's oration to the City Fathers of Athens whose special concern was the religion and education of its citizens. The conservatives take it as a verbatim report of what Paul said; the radicals, with a colossal assurance that always amazes us, declare, 'Paul could never have spoken like this'. What is the real truth?

Luke was not with Paul during his brief stay in Athens. His account cannot therefore be a *Hansard* report of the apostle's words. But to avow this is not to agree with those who say, 'The speech is Luke's invention'.

Anyone, using a concordance to the Greek New Testament, may detect in these ten verses of Acts about the same number of 'Lucanisms' – words or phrases elsewhere favoured by Luke. But it does not follow that Luke knew nothing of Paul's speech in Athens and simply 'made it up'. Why should it be thought incredible that Paul told Luke the gist of what he had said to the Athenian intelligentsia? The man who, by his own confession, could, for the gospel's sake, 'make himself all things to all men' (I Cor. 9.22), may very well have told his friend and physician that, when he stood before the Areopagites, he did just that. 'I took my cue,' we may imagine him saying, 'from an altar I had seen on my tour of Athens, and I quoted back at them their own poets.' He may well have confided to Luke, 'My speech, alas, misfired. Just when, having talked natural theology to them, I began to talk of Jesus and the resurrection, some began to scoff. But I made a few converts, a member of the learned Court among them, plus a woman named Damaris, and a few others.' So far from being incredible, we think this eminently probable.

For when you study the *Areopagitica*, making due allowance for the 'Lucanisms', you find much in it which is *echter Paulus*, genuine Paul.

To begin with, that *captatio benevolentiae* – that appeal for his hearers' goodwill:

'Men of Athens, I perceive that you are in every way very religious' (RSV: this is much likelier than the AV's 'too superstitious'. Only a fool – and Paul was no fool – would have begun with such a studied insult.)

Paul did not much like what he had seen of Athenian religion – images and idols everywhere – but their 'religiosity' he could not deny. Indeed, it is well attested from independent sources. The second-century geographer Pausanias tells us that 'the Athenians venerate their gods more than other men'. Josephus said much the same thing. Right religion it might not be for Paul, but here was a *point d'appui*, a place from which to start on this momentous occasion. From other sources we know that the Athenians liked to erect altars to 'unknown gods', and it is not impossible that Paul's eye had lighted on one inscribed: 'To an (or the) unknown God'. Here was a text in stone from which to preach. 'What you worship but do not know,' he said, 'this is what I proclaim.' To the 'agnostics' of Athens he will declare the knowledge of the one true and living God.

How does he begin? Some critics would have it that he proceeds forthwith to talk pure Stoicism, presumably to ingratiate himself with his audience; for Stoicism at that time was the dominant philosophy of the Roman Empire. Not so do we read Luke's record of Paul's speech in Acts. Five things he says: (1) God is the All-Creator (Isa. 42.5); (2) he does not dwell in man-made shrines (I Kings 8.27; Stephen had said this); (3) men do not provide for his wants but he for theirs (Ps. 50.12); (4) out of one he has made all nations, fixing their seasons and boundaries (Deut. 32.8); (5) his desire was that they should all seek and find him

(Isa. 55.6). If this is Stoicism, it is Stoicism speaking with a strong Hebrew accent!

Having entered our protest against finding Stoicism everywhere in the *Areopagitica*, let us now freely concede that the Paul of the epistles could, when it suited him, talk like a Stoic. He does so in Rom. 2.14f.:

> When Gentiles who do not have the law do by nature what the law requires ... they show that what the law requires is written in their hearts.

Tarsus was a notable centre for Stoic teachers who taught that all nature is pervaded by a divine principle, and that 'conscience' – the intuitive sense of right and wrong – is man's awareness of it. For Paul, of course, the Law, or Torah, was a higher revelation of God's nature and will than that given in the natural world; but here he accepts the Stoic view that God has not left man without some knowledge of his will and of his moral obligation, as creature, to obey it.

Another example of Paul's Stoicism is the doxology with which he ends his 'philosophy of history' in Rom. 9-11:

> All comes from him, all lives by him, all ends in him (Rom. 11.36).

Paul would never, of course, have construed these words like a Stoic. Between his doctrine of the living God and Stoic pantheism lay a world of difference. But what we are showing is that the author of Romans could 'talk Stoic'.

Now turn to the next verses of the *Areopagitica:*

> Yet God is not far from each one of us, for
> 'In him we live and move and have our being';
> as some of your poets have said,
> 'For we are indeed his offspring'
> Being then God's offspring, we ought not to think that the Deity is like gold, silver, or stone, a representation by the art and imagination of man (Acts 17.27b-29).

Here the speaker deliberately 'goes all Stoic'. A quotation from the Stoic poet Epimenedes is followed by another from Aratus who hailed, like Paul, from Cilicia. The speaker stresses the immanence of God, a doctrine dear to the Stoic but no less dear to the Christian. Men, he insists, who are God's offspring should have more sense than to worship man-made images. (Paul said this in Rom. 1.23f.)

With this the speaker's *prolegomena* on 'natural theology'

are finished. Now he begins to expound the gospel. Three things he is allowed to say:

First, if in the past God has 'overlooked men's ignorance' (which reminds us of Rom. 3.25: 'In his forbearance God had overlooked the sins of the past' NEB), he was now 'commanding all men everywhere to repent' – to turn back to God. So Paul had urged his hearers in Thessalonica to 'turn from idols, to serve a living and true God', I Thess. 1.9. And the reason why? Because, second, a new era in history has begun which is to end 'on a day when God will judge the world'. And what is this but Rom. 2.16, 'That day when, according to my gospel, God judges the secrets of men by Christ Jesus'? Third, on that day God's agent will be 'a man of his own appointing'. The 'Man' here is Jesus the Son of man – the same man, who was also God's servant, referred to by Paul in Rom. 5.12ff.[1]

The last word of the *Areopagitica* concerns the resurrection of Jesus. 'Of this (the judgment) God has given assurance to all men by raising him (the man) from the dead.' That one vacant tomb in the wide graveyard of the world was pledge and promise of the final judgment and victory of God.

So the *Areopagitica* came to an abrupt end. Had the speaker gone on to talk of the immortality of the soul (as Plato the Greek, centuries before, had done) the wiseacres of Athens would have heard him gladly. But his doctrine of the resurrection of the body – this was too much for enlightened Greeks for whom *sōma sēma*, 'the body is a tomb' and 'dead men rise up never'.

To the sceptical scholars who dismiss the whole speech as a Lucan invention, we say: Is it, after all, so unlike Paul of the Romans? Is not its tone and approach just what we might have expected from Paul in Athens, and faced with such an audience?

Of course the *Areopagitica* does not give us the full-orbed gospel of the apostle to the Gentiles. It is basically 'an introductory lesson in Christianity for cultured pagans'. Starting from their own confessed ignorance of God's true nature, it went on to discuss God in nature and providence, and ended abruptly with a brief statement of the apostolic gospel. Had the Athenian 'fathers and brethren' returned for the second lesson some wanted, Paul would surely have explained more fully how 'in Christ God was reconciling the world to himself' (II Cor. 5.19).

It was not to be. To the mass of his Greek hearers Paul's gospel was 'foolishness' (I Cor. 1.23) 'Give us wisdom,' was their cry, 'Give us an intellectually satisfying solution to the riddle of the world'. It had not dawned on them, as it has not yet dawned on our modern Greeks, that the ultimate mystery of the world is what Paul calls 'the mystery of iniquity' (II Thess. 2.7), the undeniable and intractable reality of original sin which thwarts and blights all man's best endeavours, and with which no act of parliament can cope.

Had the Athenians come back for a second session, Paul might have told them (as he did the Corinthians) that the only thing which makes sin and moral evil intelligible is not some philosophy excogitated by human wisdom but a new revelation of reality given in a mighty act of God in history, the cross and its tremendous sequel. For there, if we will read the event with Christian eyes, we see the very God himself entering into the situation our human sin has created and, by taking the burden of it upon himself, enabling us also to overcome and find the secret of new, victorious life. Here is 'wisdom' for a world baffled by moral evil; here at last sin gets a meaning as a foil to divine grace; here we see the Almighty himself, in Christ, redeeming sinful men by loving them to the uttermost:

> The very God! Think, Abib, dost thou think?
> So the All-Great were the All-loving too:
> So, through the thunder comes a human voice,
> Saying, 'Oh heart I made, a heart beats here!
> Face, my hands fashioned, see it in Myself.
> Thou hast no power, nor mayst conceive of Mine;
> But love I gave thee, with Myself to love,
> And thou must love Me, who have died for thee.'[2]

NOTES

1. In Rom. 5.12ff., 'Paul united the two basic concepts of the Son of Man and the Servant of God exactly as Jesus united them.' O. Cullmann, *The Christology of the New Testament*, SCM Press 1959, pp. 170ff.

2. Browning, 'The Epistle of Karshish'.

21

The Lord and the Apostle

Was Paul the supreme interpreter of Jesus and his gospel, or was he its greatest corrupter?

It is an old question, much discussed these last hundred years. C. S. Lewis[1] believed it was all part of a movement meant to discredit Christ himself:

> In the early history of every rebellion there is a stage at which you do not yet attack the King in person. You say, 'The King is all right. It is his Ministers who are wrong. They misrepresent him and corrupt all his plans – which, I'm sure, are good plans if only the Ministers would let them take effect.' And the first victory consists in beheading a few Ministers: only at a later stage do you go on and behead the King himself. In the same way, the nineteenth-century attack on St Paul was really only a stage in the revolt against Christ.

In the last century the most notable vilifier of the apostle was Ernest Renan. Prophesying that the day of 'the ugly little Jew' was over, he went on to say: 'The writings of Paul have been a peril and a stumbling-block, the cause of the principal defects of Christian theology.'

Even today the delusion dies hard, especially among those who pontificate in realms where their writ does not run. Thus, a few years ago, in a book *What I Believe*, Lord Robert Boothby made bold to write:

> Paul clapped humanity into chains from which Jesus had freed himself ... and substituted a religion of death for a religion of life, a religion of slavery to sin for a religion of emancipation from it, and a religion of suffering for a religion of joy.[2]

What stuff and nonsense this is! There never was an original simple gospel of freedom and joy of the kind Lord Boothby imagines. It was Christ himself who put the cross in it, and so far from clapping humanity in chains, none did more than Paul – witness *Galatians* – to break the Jewish fetters which some wanted to rivet on Christ's followers.

But since such libels on St Paul are still put about, we must show, by a stated case, how false the charge is.

I

At the beginning of this century many scholars who tackled this problem stultified their whole approach to it by making a false start. Their capital mistake was the simple but serious one of comparing Jesus and Paul as religious types or personalities. When they began by asking, Had Jesus and Paul the same religion? they asked the wrong question and got the wrong answer.

It was (let us remember) the hey-day of Liberal Protestantism when the religion of Jesus could be summed up in the paternalistic theism of the Sermon on the Mount and the Lord's Prayer, and the great Liberal scholar Harnack could declare that 'the Gospel, as Jesus proclaimed it, had to do with the Father only, and not with the Son'.[3] Accordingly, when men compared the religion of Paul with the religion of Jesus, they naturally concluded that Paul had substituted a complicated religion about Jesus for an originally simple Galilean gospel. (They tended to ignore, or under-rate, the cross in which Christ's whole ministry culminated and was consummated.) By putting the person of Jesus at the centre of his religion and investing him with the trappings of dogma and mysticism Paul the perverter had transformed the Galilean gospel into a cosmic drama of redemption. So they talked of Paul as 'the second founder of Christianity'. Had he read their writings, how indignantly would Paul have repudiated that accusation!

These men made two cardinal mistakes. First, they ignored, or denied, the *Messianic* aspects of Jesus' person and work. Second, they sought to compare two really incomparable things – the Jesus of the gospels in *his historical* situation, and the apostle's Christ in *his*.

In fact, if we are to proceed scientifically, Jesus and Paul ought never to be confronted as religious types; they should be compared *in their historical relation to each other*.

Let us put it this way. Only if Paul had been a disciple of Jesus, trained in his school and primarily concerned to transmit and interpret his teaching to others, would it be logically legitimate to compare the religion of Jesus with the theology of Paul. But Paul was not such a disciple; in fact Jesus never had such a disciple. Paul, like the other apostles, was one who proclaimed the death and resurrection of Jesus as a great saving act of God (see I Cor. 15.3ff.). In their handling of this problem the Liberals made a major methodological error. The only relevant and proper question here is: *Did Paul's gospel faithfully fulfil the intention of Jesus as we know it from the gospels, or did he falsify it by abandoning all that Jesus lived and died for?*

Before we answer, let us remember that between Jesus and Paul stood the earliest church (the *Urgemeinde*, as the Germans call it). Now it is one notable achievement of modern scholarship that it has shown that, however much Paul put his own stamp upon it, in the essentials of their gospel Paul and the first apostles were at one. Thus is confirmed a claim that Paul himself made in I Cor. 15.3-11: 'But what matter I or they (Peter, John, James and the rest), this is what we all proclaim, and this is what you believe.' Did the earliest Christians – and Paul after them – fulfil or falsify the gospel of Jesus? This is the question.

II

It is the merest truth to say that, thanks to a better understanding of the eschatology of the gospels, we now know, as the Liberal Protestants did not, what Jesus' gospel really was. It was a message of 'inaugurated eschatology'. Jesus began his Galilean ministry with the proclamation that the reign of God had dawned – was 'upon them' (Mark 1.15). God had begun to take to himself his great power and reign. That reign was being realized in himself and his ministry which was the campaign of the kingdom of God against the kingdom of evil. Calling himself the Son of Man (a cryptic name for the Messiah) he saw his God-appointed destiny as that of the Lord's Suffering Servant (Isa. 53). Moreover, he saw his ministry as moving inexorably to a supreme crisis which would involve not only judgment on old Israel and his own death for men's deliverance but also his victory over death and the rise of a new people of God.

Finally, that crisis he saw against the background of a

final consummation when God would complete his saving work in grace and judgment. In that conviction Jesus went to the cross and, as the New Testament goes on to tell, to his triumph.

When we turn to Paul, we find that he too looks forward to a final consummation (the *Parousia*, or royal coming of Christ), but just as surely he *looks back* to the cross and resurrection of Jesus as a finished work of God through which believers in the risen Christ may gain forgiveness and new life, be numbered among God's new people, and receive the power and guidance of the Holy Spirit.

Thus Paul's theology (and with it the *kērygma* of the first Christians) is *faith's answer* to the saving work of God which Jesus proclaimed, embodied and effected, and between Jesus and Paul there emerges a deep, fundamental continuity.

Yet, if there is continuity, there is also difference between them. Jesus goes to the cross as *Viator*, as one who presses forward to the goal, not as one who has reached it (*Comprehensor*), as the pilgrim Son of God who travels by faith the road appointed by his Father. *Per contra*, Paul, the herald of the risen Lord, looks back on Christ's finished journey and all the blessings it has brought. The difference between Jesus and Paul is the difference of situations before and after Easter and Pentecost. What differentiates Paul and the first Christians from Jesus is that for them the new age has come in power with the death, resurrection and exaltation of Jesus. With these events the period of the Law is over (cf. Luke 16.16 with Rom. 10.4); the righteousness of God ('God's way of righting wrong') has become a *fait accompli*; the new ecclēsia of God has become a reality; and 'in Christ' Christians become sons of God, enjoying even now a foretaste of the final salvation of God.

This point about continuity-cum-difference may be made in another way.

The apostles' *kērygma*[4] contained three essential statements: (1) The prophecies are fulfilled; (2) the new age has come with the coming of Christ; (3) therefore repent and believe.

Jesus' proclamation likewise had three parts: (1) The prophecies are fulfilled; (2) the reign of God has dawned; (3) therefore repent and believe.

In both *kērygmas* items (1) and (3) are identical. But if

we examine item (2), we find that the proclamation of the ministry, death and resurrection of Jesus has replaced his proclamation of the dawning kingdom of God. What has made the difference? The answer is of course: Easter and Pentecost. The gospel of Christ, which was the gospel of Paul and the earliest Christians, has replaced the gospel of the kingdom because by his death and resurrection Christ became the kingdom, became all that the kingdom contained. If the gospel of the kingdom was Christ in essence, Christ was the gospel of the kingdom in power. If the kingdom was Christ in a mystery, Christ was the establishment of the kingdom. He was the truth of his own great gospel, and to have him is to ensure it. As St John was to put it, 'He that has the Son has life – eternal life' (I John 5.13).

We conclude that the gospel of the earliest Christians – and of Paul after them, for they preached the same gospel (I Cor. 15.1-11) – is, if we allow for the difference made by the first Easter Day and Pentecost, the fulfilment, not the distortion, of the gospel which Jesus proclaimed. Paul and Jesus are not at variance; they are at one, and Paul can rightly claim that he has 'the mind of Christ' (I Cor. 2.16).

III

We now propose to show that in their views of man's situation before God the Lord and his apostle agree.

The very suggestion of such agreement may seem to some absurd. On what may be called 'our human predicament' they assume a wide cleavage between Jesus and Paul. They contrast the simple and glad 'religion of Jesus' with the gloomy theology of the apostle. They suppose that Jesus held fairly optimistic views of man and his 'salvability' is in contrast with Paul's sombre doctrines of man's guilt and God's wrath.

To show how false is this antithesis, let us begin by noting that *in their attitude to the Law* the contrast is chimerical.

For both, *the Law is the revelation of God's will.* Jesus assumes its validity and truth. When he is asked, 'What must I do to inherit eternal life?' he replies, 'You know the commandments' (Mark 10.17ff.). Challenged to name 'the chief commandment', he points to Deut. 6.4f. and Lev. 19.18 (Mark 12.29ff.). And he declares that he has come not to abolish the Law and the Prophets but to 'fulfil' them (Matt. 5.17).

Paul likewise holds the Law to be the revelation of God's will for men. Though he says that since the coming of faith the Law *as a system of salvation* is finished (Gal. 3.23ff.), he declares that the Law is 'holy' and 'spiritual', and the commandment 'holy and just and good' (Rom. 7.12-14). And he agrees that he who fulfils the Law gains life (Rom. 2.10; 10.5).

Next, both Jesus and Paul lay the emphasis on the *moral* demands of the Law. It is to these, 'You shall not commit murder' etc., that Jesus directs the rich young ruler (Mark 10.17ff.). He plays off the fifth commandment against the Scribes and Pharisees who practise Corban (Mark 7). And he singles out 'justice, mercy and good faith' as 'the weightier matters of the Law' (Matt. 23.23). Paul's approach is the same. When, discussing the Law, he has to choose a concrete example, he takes the tenth commandment, the only one which deals with inward impulse rather that overt act (Rom. 7.7). No less significantly in Rom. 2.14f. he regards the Gentiles' 'conscience' – the moral law within – as their equivalent for the Jewish Law.

Finally, both Jesus and Paul take *the commandment of love* to *be the core and essence of the Law*. Compare Mark 12.29-31 with Rom. 13.8-10 'Love is the fulfilling of the Law'.

But does not Paul say that the Law drives man to sin, and declare that God's grace alone, and not works of law can save men (Gal. 2.16)? He does indeed; yet he does not say that works are not God's will – quite the contrary! 'We are God's workmanship, created in Christ Jesus *for* good works' (Eph. 2.10). What Paul means is that every attempt to *earn* salvation is not only foredoomed to failure but is presumptuous sin against God (Rom. 10.3f.).

Though his language differs, the view of Jesus is the same. The servant who has 'done the things commanded' has 'no cause for boasting'. So we also, he says in the story of the Farmer and his Man (Luke 17.7-10), when we have done our duty, must own ourselves 'unworthy servants'. 'Is it enough to forgive an offending brother seven times?' Peter asks his Master hopefully. 'No, seventy times seven!' comes the answer. There is no 'enough' with God. And in his parable of the Good Employer (Matt. 20.1-15) Jesus shows

that for the legalist in religion God's sheer grace to undeserving men must ever remain a nonsense.

But the parallel between Jesus' teaching and Paul's does
not end there.

Consider next the doctrine of *justification by faith*. If
anything has a right to be called Pauline, surely this has.
If a man would 'get right with God', Paul says, he must
renounce any attempt to establish his own righteousness
before God and, owning his unworthiness, cast himself upon
God's forgiving grace in Christ. Surely on an issue like this
there is a great gulf between the Lord and his apostle!

There is not: on this theological principle they are at
one. Take the greatest of Christ's parables (Luke 15.11-32).
Without a word of lawcourt language, it teaches precisely
what Paul means by 'justification' or 'acquittal', and its message can be summed up in a phrase of Paul's 'God who
acquits the guilty' (Rom. 4.5). If we ask, What does the parable teach about God? the answer is, God is a God of sheer
grace – the God who freely forgives the man who has no
claim on his forgiveness, who can only say 'I have sinned
against heaven and before you; I am no longer worthy to be
called your son'. If we ask next, What does the parable teach
about man's salvation? the answer is, Not by works (this
was the elder brother's plea) but by a heart-felt confession
of his own unworthiness and a casting of himself on God's
mercy, is a man saved. Rightly do Sanday and Headlam
say,[5] 'Reduced to its simplest elements, justification is simply
free forgiveness. The parable of the Prodigal Son is a picture
of it.'

Now let us compare the Beatitudes of Jesus (Matt. 5.3-10)
with I Cor. 1.26-31. Jesus pronounces God's blessing on 'those
who know their need of God', 'the mourners', 'the humble'
and those who 'hunger and thirst to see right prevail' – in
a word, on all the lowly and despised of this world who,
knowing their own insufficiency, rest all their hope on God.
Do not the Beatitudes find a true spiritual echo in what Paul
says to the 'saints' of Corinth? 'Think,' he says, 'what sort
of people you are whom God has called: not many wise, by
worldly standards, not many powerful, not many of noble
birth. But God chose what is low and despised in this world,
so that no human being might boast in the presence of God.'

Take finally the parable of the Pharisee and the Tax-collector (Luke 18.9-14). Not the Pharisee who parades his own religious achievements before God, but the tax-collector who cries out of a deep sense of his unworthiness, 'God be merciful to me, a sinner!' is justified (*dedikaiōmenos*) in God's sight. This is not merely Paul's doctrine; it is his very word. The apostle's doctrine of justification goes back to Jesus.

One more argument can be thrown into the scale of proof. Paradoxical though it sounds, it is true to say that *the Sermon on the Mount and the Epistle to the Romans belong together – concur in their conviction that we are united in our status as sinners before God.*

This is a hard saying, if we stick to the concordance and study words only. In Romans Paul has much to say about sin (as a personified force, with a capital S); Jesus, if we count only specific words for sin, little or nothing in his Sermon.

In any appraisal of our Lord's attitude to sin, we can begin by listing the actual sins which he condemned – pride, hypocrisy, ingratitude, lack of compassion, the unforgiving spirit. Or we can pick out sayings like 'If you, then, being evil . . .' where Jesus quietly assumes 'the corruption of man's heart'. Yet we shall never understand how seriously he accounted sin till we see that his view of it is *an inference from his view of righteousness*. Here the Sermon supplies the best evidence, especially the six great antitheses of Matt. 5.21-48, in which Jesus sets forth the contrast between the Law of Moses as a code of commandments to be carried out, and God's true will for men. As of old Isaiah 'saw the Lord high and lifted up' and realized his own unrighteousness, so we may suppose the men on whose ears and hearts fell the revelation of God's holy will in the Sermon, saw the divine ideal and knew how far they fell short of it. The Sermon is the most damning indictment of human sin in literature. 'There is no account of sin to match the Sermon.'[6] Who is sufficient to meet its towering demands? If that is how God means his children to live, we may well say with the tax-collector 'God be merciful to us, sinners!'

In Jesus' teaching, then, 'no one is good' by God's standards. Anger, desire, hatred, vengefulness, all are transgressions of God's will. If we succumb to them, as we do, there is nothing left but to consent with Paul 'There is none who does good, no, not one' (Rom. 3.12).

Jesus does not use the vocabulary or thought-forms of his apostle, as he does not speculate about sin's origin or psychologize about its workings. But in their conviction that we are united in our status as sinners before God, and that his grace avails not for the self-righteous but for penitent sinners, they are at one.

To sum up. It is false to say that Paul preached a different gospel from Jesus. It is the same *Heilstat Gottes* – the same saving act of God – which is the central theme of both the gospels and the epistles. But whereas Jesus, who not only announces but embodies this *Heilstat*, speaks of it as *Viator* on this side of Calvary, Paul speaks of it from the vantage-point of Easter and Pentecost, proclaims its effectuation 'in power' by the resurrection and the gift of the Spirit. More-over, it is false to say that in their views of sin and salvation Jesus and Paul are at variance: different as their words, images and concepts may be, they are in basic agreement.

Yet there is one quite decisive difference between them, and none realized it better than Paul himself. It is this: Jesus knows himself to be the Christ of God, the bringer to men of God's final salvation; Paul is but the servant and envoy of this Christ. The difference between Jesus and Paul is that suggested by the title of this essay. Paul is the apostle; Jesus is the Lord.

NOTES

1. In his preface to J. B. Phillips, *Letters to Young Churcnes*, 1947 Fontana ed., p. x.

2. G. Unwin (ed.), *What I Believe*, Allen & Unwin 1966, p. 39.

3. A. Harnack, *What is Christianity?*, 1900, p. 144.

4. For a full account of the apostles' *kērygma* see the last essay in this book, pp. 178ff. below.

5. W. Sanday and A. C. Headlam, *Romans*, International Critical Commentaries ³1898, p. 36.

6. C. Ryder Smith, *The Biblical Doctrine of Salvation*, 1941, p. 170.

22

Paul the Liberator
Galatians

'It is not for glory, riches or honour that we fight,' said the
Scots to the Pope in 1320, 'but for that liberty which no
good man will lose but with his life.' In the fight for Christian
freedom some twelve centuries earlier none strove more
valiantly than Paul. The letter we know as Galatians is a
sword-stroke in his battle, and upon his winning it hung,
humanly speaking, the future of Christianity. It is not an
easy letter to read, and sometimes Paul's arguments from
the Old Testament may well leave us cold. But, like other
people's, Paul's arguments are less important than the conclusion which he reaches, which is that we must never allow
the gospel to get tangled up with Jewish legalism.

Who were the Galatians? Possibly folk of Gallic origin in
the ancient kingdom of Galatia (near modern Ankara); much
more probably, as Sir William Ramsay argued, dwellers in
the Roman province of Galatia – the Christians in Derbe,
Lystra, Iconium etc., whom Paul had evangelized on their
first missionary journey (Acts 13-14).

Some time after the two apostles left, there had arrived in
Galatia some Jewish Christians – 'Judaizers' we call them
for short – telling Paul's converts that, if they wanted to be
proper Christians, they must be circumcized and keep the
Law of Moses – in other words, become Jews before they
became Christians. Paul, they insinuated, was only a second-
hand apostle, having derived all he knew about Christ from
Peter and the original apostles in Jerusalem. Besides, he
was a trimmer, saying one thing here and another there
when the Law was in question.

When news reached Paul that the Galatians had fallen
for this Judaized travesty of the gospel, he 'saw red'. 'I am

astonished to find you turning away so quickly from him who
called you in his grace' he wrote, 'You gormless Galatians,
who has bewitched you?' Read the letter in a modern translation, and you will understand why men like J. B. Phillips,
when turning it into contemporary English, have felt like
men re-wiring an old house 'with the mains turned on'.

I

Galatians has six chapters. In the first two, which are
autobiographical, Paul defends his gospel and his apostolic
credentials. To rebut the slanders of the Judaizers, he tells
the story of his life: how as a perfervid Pharisee he had
once harried the Christians until that day on the Damascus
Road when God had revealed his Son to him, and called him
to be an apostle to the Gentiles; how on later visits to Jerusalem the 'pillar' apostles there had acknowledged his
apostleship, endorsed his gospel, approved his mission; how,
later still, at Antioch, he Paul had been forced to rebuke
the 'rock' apostle, Peter himself, for betraying what he knew
to be the liberty of the gospel and leading others astray.

In chapters 3 and 4, which are *doctrinal*, Paul makes three
appeals. His first is to the Galatians' Christian experience.
'Was it by keeping the Law,' he asks, 'or by believing the gospel
that you received God's Spirit and all those wonderful
visitations of his grace? Answer me – honestly.'

Second, he appeals to scripture. 'Go back to Genesis,' Paul
says, 'and you will see that it was not by Law-keeping but
by faith that Abraham found acceptance with God and the
promise that in himself and his seed all nations would be
blessed. It is the men of *faith* who are his true sons · and
share in his promised blessing. Scripture itself says that
trying to save yourself by Law-keeping brings only curse
and condemnation, since no man can fully keep the Law.
From that condemnation Christ bought us freedom when,
on the cross, God made him a curse for us. The Law, which
came four centuries after Abraham, was an after-thought in
the working out of the divine purpose. Its real effect was to
deepen sin by exposing it as transgression. Think of it as a
child guardian ('pedagogue') leading us to Christ, so that
through him we might get right with God by faith.

Once we resembled the heir to an estate while yet a minor.
Kept under ward, his status differs little from a slave's. But

a day dawns when he comes of age and into his inheritance. Just so, we once lived in bondage to false gods. But, when his appointed time came, God sent his own Son to deliver us from the Law's bondage and make us his adopted sons. And the proof that in union with Christ we are such, is his Spirit in our hearts moving us to call God Abba Father. Why then do you want to revert to that sorry slavery from which Christ has freed you?'

Paul's third appeal is to the time when first he had gone among the Galatians with the gospel. Then they had welcomed him, ill and unprepossessing though he was, as a messenger from heaven for whom they would have given their very eyes. 'What has come over you,' he cries, 'O my little children, must I be in birth pangs all over again till Christ takes shape in you?'

In chapters 5 and 6, which are *practical*, Paul says, 'The freedom Christ has won for you never surrender! To submit to circumcision and try to make yourselves right with God by Law-keeping is to sever your connexion with Christ and fall from grace. The one thing needful is faith – faith active in love.

I am confident that despite your set-back, whoever caused it, you will yet run well. But, as you are free men, never let your freedom become licence to indulge your lower nature. Serve one another with that love which sums up the whole Law. The way to overcome your lower nature is to let God's Spirit lead you and produce in you his gracious fruits – love, joy, peace and all the rest.

If a man does wrong, correct him gently, for none of us is .immune to temptation. And bear each other's burdens, so fulfilling the law of Christ. God is not to be fooled. As a man sows, he reaps. Sow to your lower nature, and you will reap a deadly harvest. Sow in the Spirit's field, and you will reap eternal life. Therefore never tire of doing good.

Here is my parting word to you, written in my own bold capitals.

The sole aim of these circumcizing brethren is to glory in the number of their converts and escape persecution for the cross of Christ. But God forbid that I should glory in anything but that cross which has changed the world for me! What counts is neither circumcision nor uncircumcision but men re-created in Christ.

From now on let none trouble me, for I carry on my scarred body the marks of my Owner, Jesus. His grace be with you all.'

II

The main question in Galatians is: How does a man become a Christian – by works of Law or by faith in Christ?

Originally, works of Law had meant devotion to God as expressed in the Ten Commandments. But, by Paul's day, Jewish religion had, like Molière's ghost, improved very much for the worse! As their theologians, the Scribes, kept 'fencing the Law', the number of the Commandments had grown and grown till now they numbered six hundred and thirteen. Thus the soul went out of religion. Instead of heart-to-heart communion with the living God, it became the observance of a host of vexatious rules and regulations, on the punctilious keeping of which salvation depended. God was turned into a great Taskmaster whose rules were hard to remember and harder still to observe. And if, like Paul before his conversion you were an earnest Pharisee, you ended up, as he did, with a cry of utter despair (Rom. 7.24).

Here we may recall how Christ himself castigated the Scribes and Pharisees for binding grievous legal burdens on men's shoulders, getting their moral priorities all wrong, and shutting men out of God's kingdom (Matt. 23). 'Away with this hypocrisy!' he had said. 'The whole Law is summed up in two commandments – love God with all your heart and love your neighbour as yourself' (Mark 12.29-31). 'Come to me, all you who are labouring under the Law's heavy burdens, and I will give you rest' (Matt. 11.28).

And when Paul met Christ, he found it was true: salvation is by faith in Christ, and not by works of Law.

By faith or by works? Is not this just an ancient controversy now as dead as the dodo? No, indeed! It keeps recurring in church history. Is not in fact salvation by works the creed of many a modern man? Ask him what religion means to him, and his answer will be not unlike the Pharisee's in Christ's parable (Luke 18.9-14): 'I keep the Ten Commandments – or most of them. I don't cheat in business or injure other people. I'm not an extortioner or an adulterer or, for that matter, like that publican I could name. I may not keep Lent or tithe my income for the support of the church. But I respect religion. I even take communion twice a year. So I'm quite happy with my little code of rules, and at the Last Judgment – if there is one – I don't think the Almighty will have much against me.'

How far all this falls short of what Paul means by being a Christian! Is it not, basically, the modern version of salvation by works – a few works at any rate?

What makes a man a Christian? Is it the observance of rules and regulations or that self-commitment to God's Son which is called faith? Codes of conduct, rules and regulations, may have their necessary place in life, and their function may not be so negative and null as Paul supposes. The trouble is that they do not go to the root of the matter – the part which makes us right or wrong. True change of heart in a man can never be effected by regulating conduct from without. At best, such regulating will produce a tamed animal – not a new man. What is needed to cleanse and change a man's heart is what Thomas Chalmers called 'the expulsive power of a new affection' – falling in love with God's Saviour Son, and staying in love with him, and serving others in love for his sake, till you can say with something of Paul's great simplicity. 'The life I now live in the flesh I live by faith in the Son of God who loved me and gave himself for me.' (Gal. 2.20.) This, in Paul's view, is what is meant by faith, this it is which makes a man a Christian.

Thus (to sum up) in his letter to those 'gormless Galatians' long ago Paul was really contending for the very truth and liberty of the gospel. If he had lost the battle, the gospel might have been put into a legal strait-jacket, Christianity might have dwindled away into a heretical sect of Judaism, and Paul's vision of a world-wide church of Christ (as he expounds it, for example, in Ephesians) become an empty dream.

Nor is 'the epistle of Christian freedom' a dead letter today. Soul-destroying legalism of one sort or another can still rear its ugly head in the modern church. When this happens – whenever the observance of a code of pettifogging rules and regulations is set on a level with trust in Christ as the condition of salvation – Galatians can become again (what it was in Luther's hands at the Reformation) a sword of the Spirit to strike the error down. Christ's is the only name given under heaven whereby men may be saved, and trust in him as Saviour – a trust that works through love – the only way of salvation.

23

Paul the Theologian

Romans

The word 'theology' is apt to put the modern man off. He supposes it to mean some high-flown 'God Talk' which has little or no relation to real life or the many problems which vex us today. Some theology is undoubtedly like that. Lucubrated in academic bowers, it knows little of the pang, the tragedy, the crisis of the actual world at large, with its sin and guilt. Yet, basically, theology is 'faith thinking', faith giving a reasoned account of itself, in answer to the problems which life poses. And it is in Romans, his *magnum opus*, that we find Paul doing just this. Romans is in fact the answer to the question, What is Christianity? by the greatest thinker in the early church; it is an answer validated in real experience; and what Paul says in Romans is very much our business.

I

Romans has sixteen chapters. The last one, which is mostly a list of names, we can here omit. For our purpose we may also dwell briefly on chapters 9-11, a part of the letter which may well have been composed earlier by the apostle. It deals with what we may call 'the Jewish Question'. Here Paul faces the problem over which he had long agonized: 'Why have the Jews, God's own people – my own people – rejected Jesus their Messiah and apparently excluded themselves from the grace of God?'

First (9), looking at the problem from the divine side, he says (overstressing, admittedly, the sovereignty of God): 'God is sovereign Lord of history and may do just as he wills.' Next (10), he surveys it from the human angle, saying, 'The

Jews have only themselves to blame. They have gone the wrong way about salvation – seeking to save themselves and rejecting God's grace in Christ.' But he cannot rest in this sad conclusion, and in his last word on the subject (11), he holds out the mysterious hope that Israel, which has presently lost its high calling, will yet, when God's high purpose is complete, find his mercy.

Now let us focus on chapters 1-8 and 12-15 which contain the quintessence of Paul's gospel.

After a greeting to the Roman Christians, Paul tells them of his long-cherished wish to visit Rome. 'I am not ashamed of the gospel,' he says, 'to the man of faith it is God's power for saving sinners'; and Rome, he implies, has no lack of these.

From this point on (1.17), we may divide his letter into three parts:

(1) The Sin of Man (1.17-3.20)
(2) But the Grace of God in Christ (3.21-8.39)
(3) Therefore the Christian Ethic (12.1-15.33)

'In the gospel,' Paul begins, 'the righteousness of God is being revealed.' Here is one of his key-phrases, to be interpreted dynamically. The NEB rightly renders it 'God's way of righting wrong'. It denotes not so much a divine attribute as a divine *activity*. It means 'God putting things right for his people'. Through long centuries Israel had prayed that God would so 'put things right' for them, would intervene decisively in history to 'visit and redeem his people'. Now, Paul says, in the events that make up the gospel story – in the life, death and resurrection of Christ and the advent of the Spirit – God is to be seen doing just this.

But why is 'the righteousness of God' needed? Because of 'the unrighteousness of men'. All men, Jews and Gentiles alike, have sinned by breaking God's Law. But surely the Gentiles never had a Law to break? Yes, they had – God's Law written in their consciences, an innate sense of right and wrong. Why, you have only to look around at Gentile society, with its worship of false gods degenerating into obscene immoralities, to see God's retribution falling on their sin. Lose the true God, and that is the morass of iniquity into which you sink. But the Jews are not one whit better. God has revealed his will to them in the Law of Moses (the *Torah*) – the Ten Commandments and the rest –

and they have consistently flouted it. Thus all men, without exception, are sinners before God, as the scriptures say (1.17-3.20).

Such is the disease, sin wide as the world and deep as human nature. But 'where sin abounded, grace did much more abound'. So, at Rom. 3.21, Paul turns to the divine remedy. Now God has begun to 'put things right' for sinners. On his side, it is a matter of his gracious giving; on man's, of his unmeritorious receiving. In Christ and his atoning cross God has provided a way for guilty men to be 'justified' – to 'get right' with him. For by works of the Law (which only brings knowledge of sin) – by his own moral achievements – no man can put himself right with God.

This 'justification by God's grace through faith' is as old as Abraham, the man who took God at his word and so found acceptance with him (Gen. 15.6). Christian faith means taking God at his living and delivering word in Christ – the Christ who died and rose for our saving. When we do this, God 'sets us right' with himself, forgives us, we are reconciled to God, and we exult in hope of future glory. As from the first Adam came sin and death for his descendants, so from Christ the second Adam, come 'acquittal and life' for all who put their trust in him (4-5).

This new life means deliverance from sin's dominion, symbolized in baptism which admits us to God's people, the church. There, symbolically, we die with Christ our Saviour to our old bad life and rise into a righteous new one, as we are called to become the new men we now potentially are. It means also rescue from the death-grip which the Law gets on us through sin's power in our lower nature. Once, Paul confesses, I knew that experience only too well. Then, praise be to God, he rescued me through Christ (6-7).

Thus what the Law could not do, God has done in another way, through Christ and the cross. With our sins now forgiven, we have peace with God, his Holy Spirit is working in us shaping us to the likeness of his Son; and though suffering is still our lot, it is not worth comparing with the glory God has in store for the perfected family of God.

How shall we sum it up? With God for us, who can be against us? Not Christ (our only conceivable condemner) who has died for us and now intercedes for us in heaven! Therefore I am persuaded that neither death nor life, no power in the universe, no terror time may hold, no influence of the stars in their courses, nor anything else in all creation will be able to separate us from God's love in Christ (8).

But 'in the New Testament religion is grace and ethics gratitude' (Erskine of Linlathen). So now, in chapters 12-15, Paul describes the kind of Christian behaviour which ought to be our grateful response to God's grace. It is a life lived in the community of which Christ is the living head. As 'limbs' in his working body (Paul says) let all use their varying gifts for the common good. Be patient in trials, keep praying, be open-handed to the needy, bless your persecutors, repay no man evil for evil, but leave retribution to the Lord. (How reminiscent this is of the Sermon on the Mount!) Obey the civil authorities as ordained by God, lead law-abiding lives, pay your taxes. The highest kind of Christian conduct is love: because it injures nobody, it fulfils the whole Law.

Then Paul sounds a *reveille*. God's new day is breaking! Off then with the deeds of darkness, and on with the moral habits of Christ your Lord!

Should differences arise among you about meat-eating or observing holy days, the stronger should make allowance for their weaker brothers' scruples. To God we will all have to answer. Therefore consult your neighbour's good and build up the common life. Christ has accepted us all. Let us accept each other (12.1-15.13).

Paul closes with news of his travel plans and greetings to his friends in Rome. Pray for me, he says, that I may come to you in the fulness of the gospel, and the God of peace be with you.

II

The sin of man, *but* the grace of God, *therefore* the Christian ethic – such is the gospel as Paul expounded it to his Roman readers.

That Rome in AD 57 needed radical moral and spiritual renewal admits of no dispute. 'The sinful city on the seven hills' men called her. Of her greatest man, Julius Caesar, the Roman historian Suetonius tells us: 'He was every woman's man, and every man's woman.' For all her might and magnificence she teemèd with sin. She might bestride the world like a Colossus; she might spread her conquests from the Euphrates to the Thames; but she could do nothing to cleanse and regenerate the victims of lust and sin with which her realms were filled. All Rome's pomp and splendour lay under the divine decree that sin brings death – must end in ruin – unless God could somehow provide a cure.

Are we not in much the same spiritual plight today? What a clever creature is twentieth-century man! What mastery over the material world he can claim! Can he not capture the wandering voices of the ether in a tiny transistor, and split the atom to release illimitable sources of energy, and plant his gleaming space-ships in the immensities of God's universe!

Ah but this is only one side of the medal and, alas, the other side will hardly bear inspecting. The truth is that modern man, for all his cleverness, is a tragic figure. He prostitutes his great gifts for the production of bombs which may dissolve the world in nuclear holocaust. He befuddles himself with drink and drugs, and under their influence commits crimes of which 'the lower creation' might be ashamed. His splendid cities abound with thugs and gangsters, and vice and violence make the headlines of the news. Nor is the corruption confined to the slum and the slum-dweller. It spreads to the highest places in government, as it no less infects 'big business'. Many things modern man can do. One thing – and that the most needful of all – he cannot. He cannot save himself from his sins.

Is there then no hope for our human race? On the contrary, Paul answers, it is just here that the gospel comes in. In the gospel we have God's historic assurance to sinful man that he has not left him to 'stew in his own juice', to perish in his sinning, but is resolved upon his rescue.

What Paul said in the first century is as true now as then. The gospel of God's grace to sinners in the cross remains 'the power of God unto salvation' for every man ready to take him at his living word in Christ. Here is divine assurance that for his sin there is forgiveness, for his hurt there is healing, and for his troubled heart peace.

Some day – and, hopefully, sooner rather than later – we are going to realize that the deep sickness of our society is never to be effectively cured by higher education, by improved psychological techniques, or by politician's panacea. Why? Because at the root of all our trouble lies 'original sin' – the pride and greed and wickedness of men. With this no act of parliament can cope:

> The heart ay's the part ay
> That makes us right or wrang,

and it is there, within us, as Christ declared (Mark 7), that the trouble lies. For this 'heart' disease there is but one remedy, that gospel which Paul calls 'the power of God unto salvation to everyone that believeth'.

24

Paul the Pastor

I Corinthians

When the minister in mufti on the train told his travelling companion, a shepherd, that he was 'something of a shepherd himself', the other asked, 'What size is your flock?' 'About two thousand.' 'Man,' said the shepherd, 'you must have a fell job at the lambing time.'

Paul was a great spiritual shepherd, but what 'a fell job' he had with his flock in Corinth! That cosmopolitan Greek city, to which he had brought the gospel about AD 50, had became a byword for what today we call 'permissiveness'. Indeed, to 'Corinthianize' was polite Greek for to 'go to the devil' with womanizing, and to gather a Christian flock in it must have been like trying to set up the City of God in Vanity Fair. But set up it had been and, after Paul's departure, along had come Apollos to continue the good work. Now, some five years later, however, weeds had begun to appear among the wheat.

Some Christian travellers from Corinth had reported to Paul, now working in Ephesus, that factions were splitting the congregation, immorality was rife, and some members were carrying their quarrels into heathen law-courts. About the same time Paul got a letter from the Corinthian church itself, inviting his comments on various problems including marriage, the eating of food which had been sacrificed to idols, attendance at pagan supper parties, the value of different 'spiritual gifts' and the nature of life in the world to come.

First Corinthians is Paul's answer to the matters mentioned in the report and the questions raised in the church letter. Here is the NEB's five-fold division of its contents:

(1) Church unity and order (1-6)

(2) The Christian in a pagan society (7-11)
(3) Spiritual Gifts (12-14)
(4) Life after death (15)
(5) Christian Giving (16).
Let us paraphrase what Paul says.

I

'Dear friends in Corinth, while I thank God for all your
Christian gifts and witness, I am perturbed by a report of
serious divisions among you, one man saying, "I am for
Paul", another "I am for Apollos", a third "I am for Peter",
and a fourth "I belong to Christ". Is Christ in fragments?
Was it in Paul's name you were baptized? Was Paul crucified for you?

The cross shows that God's wisdom is not man's wisdom,
nor are God's values man's, as witness your own calling by
him. There is a wisdom which God gives to men who have
his Spirit. But when you tolerate these divisions, how quite
unspiritual you show yourselves to be! One foundation only
is there for Christian faith, Christ himself; and we apostles,
building on it, are but his servants. God's holy building
you are, and anyone who wrecks it commits sacrilege. Therefore stop exalting one human leader against another, and
please remember what your vaunted spiritual enrichment
is costing us apostles in outrage and despising from men.
Many tutors in Christ you may have, but only one father;
and when I re-visit you, it will be yours to decide whether
our meeting is fierce or gentle.

Next, I hear reports of immorality among you, including a
case of incest. Excommunicate the evil-doer forthwith, and
shun all Christians who lead loose lives.

Finally, some of you, I hear, are suing each other in pagan
law-courts. Are there not Christian judges among you fit to
settle these quarrels of yours? Better still, why not endure
injury without seeking redress? (1-6).

Now about the questions in your letter. You ask whether,
in present circumstances, a Christian should marry, and
whether a Christian may seek divorce if the marriage partner
is a pagan. My answer is: remain unmarried, if you can. If
you cannot, then marry. Divorce followed by re-marriage is
not permitted (this is our Lord's ruling). If a widow is to

be remarried, let it be to a Christian.

Next, concerning meat which has been offered to idols and attendance at pagan supper parties. "All things are lawful for a Christian," some of you are saying. Yes, but not all things are advisable. Of course these idols don't really exist – there is only one God and only one Saviour. Nevertheless, you must be ready to renounce your Christian rights if the exercise of them shocks your less enlightened brothers who worry about eating such doubtful food.

As an apostle of Christ I have as much right as any man to take a wife or be maintained by the church; but rather than hinder the gospel I refuse to exercise it. It is foolish to suppose that because you have the Christian sacraments you can safely eat sacrificial meat at pagan festivals. The Israelites in the wilderness had their sacraments also, but God punished their idolatry. So be warned!

Should women (you ask) be veiled in church? Yes, they should. The veil symbolizes woman's subordination to man, and both social convention and nature confirm my opinion.

Report has reached me that at your common meal before communion some richer members are gorging themselves and getting drunk, while the poorer members, arriving later after work, have to go hungry. Such conduct I cannot praise. This is the Lord's Supper – not an orgy. It goes back, as I told you, to what our Lord did in the upper room at the Last Supper. Unless you have a reverent sense of what you are doing, your communions may well bring on you God's judgment (7-11).

Now I must add a word about "spiritual gifts" and their relative merits. All come from the one Spirit who dwells in the one Body, which is Christ's church. In a human body no rivalry exists among the various organs. All are needed, and all work together for the common good. So it should be in the church. Far the best way of all is love, and lacking love, all gifts are nothing worth. In the world to come, they will be superseded; love alone will last on.

About "prophesying" (inspired preaching in plain words) and "speaking with tongues" (emotional utterances in words not intelligible to the ordinary hearer). The trouble about "tongues" is that, unless an interpreter is present, they benefit only their possessor, and an outsider coming into church while people are talking in tongues might well take you for crackpots. By contrast, prophecy is intelligible, searches men's consciences, and builds up the church, which is what matters most. Therefore, while not forbidding "tongues", I much prefer you to prophesy. But, one speaker at a time, please, and not more than two or three at one service, and let all things be done decently and in order (12-14).

Now concerning life after death. Some of you, apparently, while not denying Christ's resurrection, cannot believe in bodily resurrection for men. This means that you have not grasped the significance of Christ's victory over death, the central fact in the gospel tradition as I delivered it to you. If bodily resurrection is impossible, there can be no risen Christ. But in fact, Christ is indisputably risen, and his triumph over death is our assurance that those who are his will share his immortal life when God winds up the scroll of history and Christ comes in glory. The body God will give us then will be a *spiritual* one, like Christ's own glorious body – as different from the present one as the grown plant is to the seed sown in earth.

Thanks be to God who gives us the victory through our Lord Jesus Christ! On with the Lord's work and never despair' (15).

II

Such (less ch. 16 which is about the relief fund for the mother church in Jerusalem and his own travel plans) is Paul's pastoral letter. When we consider how many tricky problems he had to solve, and how few Christian precedents he had to guide him, we may well marvel at his Christian wisdom. Of course, in some of his answers, e.g., when he regards marriage as almost a last resource, or forbids women to have bare heads in church, he is patently a man of his time. But to concede this is far from saying that Paul has nothing to teach us today.

What, for example, about our continuing Christian disunity? When we survey our own 'unhappy divisions', in which one man says, 'I am of Luther', a second 'I am of Calvin', a third 'I am of Wesley' and a fourth 'I belong to the true church of Christ founded on Peter the rock', can we not hear Paul across the centuries protesting, 'Is Christ divided?' and solemnly resolve to do all we can to heal the wounds in Christ's Body?

Or take the question of food offered to idols. What Paul says about such meat applies with no less force to our 'drink' problem today. There is nothing sinful and, arguably, something socially valuable, in a moderate use of alcohol (Did not our Lord himself drink fermented wine?); but its excessive use has become today a major social evil, contributing greatly not only to the staggering increase in crime but to the break-up of countless happy homes. Often it may be the bounden duty of the Christian who is not a tee-totaller to refuse 'the social glass', lest his use of it cause the downfall of a weaker brother.

Half a century ago we had no problems about 'tongues' in the modern church. But recent years have seen the rise of 'the Charismatic Movement'. These 'Neo-Pentecostalists', as they are often called, look to the re-discovery of the Holy Spirit's power (and the New Testament is unintelligible without this) as the way of defrosting 'God's frozen people' and reviving a moribund church. Our staid, conventional Western church does indeed need to re-discover and experience the Holy Spirit's life-giving power. Yet what troubles some of us who also desire the church's renewing is what troubled Paul about the old Pentecostalists in Corinth – the stress which our 'charismatic brethren' set on the gift of tongues as the chief and true sign of possession by God's Spirit. Is not the apostle's view still the best one that while we must not quench the Spirit, all spiritual gifts must aim at one thing – to upbuild the church?

III

James Moffatt once observed that, if it had not been for some irreverent behaviour at communion in Corinth, we should never have known what Paul believed about the Lord's Supper. We may go further. If some Christians at Corinth had not been exalting 'tongues' at the expense of other spiritual gifts, the world would not have had Paul's Song of Songs about Christian love (I Cor. 13). Again, if some Christians in Corinth had not entertained doubts about bodily resurrection, we should not have had the earliest and best historical evidence for Christ's resurrection, or his teaching about the 'spiritual body' which, avoiding the drawbacks of the Greek and the Hebrew views, has helped many Christians in their thinking about the nature of life after death.

Yet, pastorally speaking, perhaps the most valuable thing of all in I Corinthians is the basic principle Paul uses to solve various practical problems (party strife, tainted meat, spiritual gifts). It is that of *service in love for the upbuilding of the whole church*. If some Christians in Corinth had learned the lesson of Christian freedom only too well, they had forgotten that 'liberty is the luxury of self-discipline'. Paul supplies the needed corrective. ' "All things are permissible" you say. Yes, but not all things are good or helpful for the upbuilding of your Christian fellowship. Therefore you "libertarians" must learn to curb your much-prized freedom for the sake of your less enlightened brothers.'

Is not this Christian principle quite as valid now as then? There is a Christian way of using one's liberty: it is to see it as something to be enjoyed in the fellowship of Christ's Body, and to exercise it in such a way as will serve the brethren and build up the church. The ideal church is a living body whose strength is service and whose life-blood is love. Thus all roads lead back to I Cor. 13. The one thing a Christian has to give his neighbour is love, and the way of giving it is that of devoted unselfish service.

25

Paul the Saint

Philippians

That deeply spiritual Catholic layman, Baron Von Hügel, being asked what qualities his church looked for in those she canonized as saints, said there were four: 'Loyalty to the faith, heroism in time of testing, the power to do what ordinarily would seem humanly impossible, and radiance amid the storm and strain of life.'

It is in Philippians that Paul qualifies most clearly on the last score. Written from his Roman prison in the early 'sixties', the letter's primary purpose was to say 'Thank you' for a gift which the congregation in Philippi (a leading city of Macedonia in northern Greece) had sent him by the hand of one of their members, Epaphroditus.

I

'Dear Christians in Philippi,' Paul begins, 'my memories of you are a continual joy to me, as I pray that you keep growing in grace. My imprisonment here has really turned out to be a blessing in disguise, since it has led to more preaching of Christ, and for this I rejoice. What the future holds for me is uncertain. For myself, I am torn in two directions. If it holds death, I shall go and be with Christ, which would be best for me. Yet, for your sakes, it is probably better that I should stay on in the body. Whatever happens, stand firm for the gospel against all opponents (1).

Above all, keep united and be humble – like Christ who, though in God's form he was, became a servant upon earth and died upon a cross, so that God highly exalted him and bestowed on him the name above all names. Work out your own salvation – with God's help – and on Judgment Day I shall be proud of you. With this letter I am sending back Epaphroditus who has been critically ill, and, later, the trusty Timothy (2).

Beware of these curs among you (Judaizing Christians, as in Galatia). Once I might have boasted myself a better Jew than any of them, but all my ancestral privileges I gladly renounced when through Christ I found peace with God and had my whole life changed. Not that I now consider myself "perfect"; but like a runner I press on towards the goal for the prize of God's high calling in Christ. My aim is to be a mature Christian. Make it yours also. Have no truck with those libertines in your midst. Remember that we are a colony of heaven and await a saviour who will change our lowly bodies into glorious ones, like his own (3).

Please help these two wrangling women to make it up. Finally, all joy be yours; have no anxiety; keep saying your prayers; and take account of virtue and merit wherever you find it around you.

I was overjoyed by your practical remembrance of me. Long experience has taught me how to cope with the ups and downs of life, so that in union with Christ I am able for anything. Yet thank you for the gift – not the first you have sent me. All the brethren here send their greetings, especially those belonging to the Emperor's Establishment.

The grace of the Lord Jesus Christ be with you all (4).'

'The sum of the letter,' said the old scholar Bengel, 'is: I rejoice, and you must rejoice too.' No fewer than sixteen times do the words 'joy' and 'rejoice' occur in it, which is an average of four 'joys' per chapter. 'My joy and crown' Paul proudly calls his readers. If they will all agree among themselves as Christians should, they will 'complete his joy'. And not once but three times he bids them 'rejoice in the Lord'. It has been truly said that 'joy as a moral quality is a Christian invention'. Philippians splendidly exemplifies it. It is 'the epistle radiant with joy'. By the last of Von Hügel's 'tests' Paul is certainly a saint.

Now for his first one: 'loyalty to the faith'. The faith which Paul proclaimed was that which all the apostles proclaimed (I Cor. 15.1-11), and they libel the apostle who say otherwise. He was no corrupter of the gospel. When he speaks, as occasionally he does (Rom. 2.16; Gal. 2.2) of 'my gospel' or 'the gospel which I preach', it is the common apostolic gospel, but stamped with his own personal experience, expressed in his own thought-forms, bearing his own characteristic emphasis. Nevertheless, the Christ who is its living centre is the same Christ whom Peter and the other apostles confessed as Lord and Son of God. If in letters like Colossians and Ephesians Paul 'gives Christ the freedom of the universe', suggesting it is all there with Christ in view (as in our own day Teilhard de Chardin and Charles Raven have done), it is not because he has invented a bigger Christ, but because he has grasped the true magnitude of his person (as St John and the writer to the Hebrews also did). 'I have kept the faith' (I Tim. 4.7) said the apostle near the end of his life, and he had a right to say so.

After 'loyalty to the faith' comes 'heroism in time of testing'. Should anyone doubt Paul's title to this quality, let him read St Luke's account of Paul's courage during the great storm on the voyage to Rome (Acts 27). Better still, let him go to Paul's own letters, especially II Cor. 11.24-28. Stung into reply by the slanders of some critics in Corinth, and calling himself a fool for yielding to the temptation to boast, he lists the hardships he had undergone as an ambassador for Christ. 'Many a time,' he writes, 'I have been face to face with death. Five times the Jews gave me thirty-nine strokes with the lash. Thrice I was beaten with Roman rods. Three times I was ship-wrecked. For twenty-four hours I was adrift in the open sea.' Then he recalls the dangers from rivers, from robbers, from false friends, all the times he had gone without sleep or food and drink, suffering cold and exposure, to which external tribulations there fell to be added (he says) his daily weight of worry for all his churches.

What incomparable fortitude was Paul's for the gospel's sake! 'I reckon fortitude's the biggest thing a man can have,' says Peter Pienaar in Buchan's *Mr Standfast*, 'just to go on enduring when there's no heart or guts left in you'. Then, naming one or two men who had exhibited fortitude, he ended, 'But the head man at the job was the apostle Paul.' Precisely so: if resolute resolve to keep going in face of fearful odds is one test of sainthood, Paul passes it with flying colours.

The last of Von Hügel's tests is 'the power to do what ordinarily would seem humanly impossible. What in the first century AD might have been so described? Would it not have been the conquest, almost single-handed, of the Roman Empire for Christ? Yet something very like this was the goal Paul set himself, and how nearly he attained it before he was martyred! 'There is something astonishing in the magnitude of the task Paul set himself,' says Dean Inge, 'and in his enormous success. By his labours the future history of the world for two thousand years, and perhaps for all time, was determined.' With none of our modern means of swift and easy travel, or of communications, this dynamic little man tramped all over Asia Minor and half of Europe, making it his ambition to bring the gospel to 'places where the very name of Christ has not been heard' (Rom. 15.20). By AD 57 he had completed his preaching of the gospel from Jerusalem in the east to Illyricum (Jugoslavia) in the west (Rom. 15.19f.). And now, God willing, he was planning to proclaim it in Rome before going on to Spain. Reach Rome he did, and from his prison there continued to bear his witness (Phil. 1.12f.). Nor is it quite impossible that he set foot on Spanish soil, for Clement of Rome, writing about AD 95, says that, before Paul went to glory, he 'reached the extreme limit of the west'. And all this he accomplished in a body racked by sharp physical pain (II Cor. 12.7). If this is not to do what ordinarily would seem humanly impossible, what else is it?

II

Yet, as Paul is indisputably a saint, he is none of your statuesque and ethereal saints wearing luminous halos and invested with dubious legends. To this type of saint Paul refuses to conform – even in physical appearance; for, according to a credible tradition, he was 'short and bald, with a hooked nose and beetling brows'. Had Paul been some shadowy moral paragon, he would never, down the centuries, have been so hated by a few, or been so loved 'this side of idolatry' by a multitude who have found in him the most heroic figure in the early church and the supreme interpreter of Christ and the gospel.

Moreover, though dead and gone to glory these nineteen hundred years, he is yet posthumously, through his letters, vibrantly alive, his words still, as Luther said, 'hands and feet to carry a man away'.

'The style is the man,' and the person who emerges from

his letters is a highly-strung man with a warm heart, a sanctified common-sense, and a powerful mind which, when it rises
to the height of its theme, can utter itself in unforgettable
Christian speech. Normally tender, affectionate and quick to
'speak the truth in love', he can yet, when the truth or
liberty of the gospel is being compromised, blaze with fine
indignation. A born leader of men, something of a mystic and
yet a great man of action, he has an unshakable conviction of
the reality of things unseen and of his own choice by God
to play a decisive part in spreading the gospel in the world.
Above all, he has a complete devotion to the church's Lord:
'For me to live is Christ' (Phil. 1.21).

III

And Paul, being dead, yet speaks to us in our human
predicament today if we will but hear him. Listen to Karl
Barth, the greatest Christian thinker of our time:

> Paul, as a child of his age, addressed his contemporaries ... as
> Prophet and Apostle of the Kingdom of God, he veritably speaks
> to all men of every age ... If we rightly understand ourselves,
> our problems are the problems of Paul; and if we be enlightened
> by the brightness of his answers, those answers must be ours.[1]

For our part, we long to see the modern church forsaking
the half-gospels of the modernist preachers in our midst
and returning to the gospel of the man P. T. Forsyth well
named 'the Fifth Evangelist'. What we have in mind is no
uncritical 'fundamentalism' – there is no future or real
security in this – but a modernized gospel reared on a
Pauline foundation – a gospel which deals faithfully with
man's sin and guilt, proclaims the free grace of an almighty
Father to sinners, and has at its heart a commanding Christ
and a redeeming cross: a gospel which ever seeks to expound
these doctrines in meaningful contemporary terms, and
looks to the power of the Holy Spirit, the Lord and giver of
life, to make them real in the lives of men and women today.

NOTE

1. *The Epistle to the Romans*, Preface to the first edition 1918, ET
1933, Oxford University Press 1968 edition, p. 1.

26

Resurrection

I Cor. 15

I

However offensive it may be to modern man, the Christian hope of life after death is centred on the resurrection of the body, not the immortality of the soul (which is Greek and Platonic in origin[1]). The New Testament contains no warrant for believing that man was created immortal, that his soul, being indestructible, must therefore survive the shock of death. 'Soul' in the Bible does not mean that part of man which outlasts death. In the Old Testament it stands for the Hebrew *nephesh* which is what we are when we are alive, not what we are when we are dead. Its New Testament equivalent is *psychē* which denotes man's emotional and mental make-up, and when we die, so does our *psychē*.

'I believe,' says the Christian 'in the resurrection of the body' not, be it noted, the resurrection of the *flesh*. One main reason why modern men agree with Swinburne that 'dead men rise up never' is, I believe, because they suppose the Christian believes in 'a resurrection of relics'. No doubt some Christians still do, as they certainly did in the Middle Ages. Then it was commonly held that at the trumpet's sound on the Last Day the dead would arise from their graves in their physical bodies, to be caught up into the presence of the Great Judge. Such a belief they might not have entertained if they had remembered what Paul expressly says: 'Flesh and blood cannot inherit the kingdom of God' (I Cor. 15.30). To this the instructed modern Christian says Amen. Years ago, Archbishop William Temple, walking with two friends in the Lake District, set themselves to climb Great Gable. His two friends gained the summit first, and, looking down, beheld the portly figure of the Archbishop slowly but steadily toiling towards the top. When at last he reached it, mopping his brow, he said, 'Thank God, gentlemen, I do not believe in the resurrection of the flesh!'

But is the Christian doctrine of the resurrection so incredible as unbelieving modern man supposes?

Begin with man as man. Man alone goes to death in full awareness of what is in store for him. He is the only animal who knows that he must die. Yet, as distinct from the other animals, he thinks he was not merely made to die – he has immortal longings. It is a fact, well supported by medical evidence[2], that even when a man knows himself to be incurably ill, his thought reaches out to a future beyond the finitude of death. He cherishes the hope that, though he is doomed to sleep the sleep of death, he will yet somehow awaken from it. It is to this phenomenology of hope that the doctrine of the resurrection of the dead gives expression.

But does not this hope of life beyond death stagger all belief? No, not if we will remember what the doctrine of resurrection – which is Jewish, not Greek, and was widely held in Christ's time – really symbolizes. It is, quite simply, the idea of *awakening from slumber* (Isa. 26.19; Dan. 12.2f.). For the Pharisees of Christ's day (as distinct from the Sadducees who denied the doctrine) rising from sleep was a parable of the destiny expected for God's people at the End-time. The faithful fall asleep in death only to awake, at God's mighty touch, on the great day. Was this, after all, so incredible a fancy for men who believed in a living God with whom in life they held communion? To adapt the last line of Blanco White's celebrated sonnet:

If light can thus deceive, wherefore not death?

For a third point, the doctrine of the resurrection of the body (unlike the Greek doctrine of the immortality of the soul) does not dichotomize man into soul and body. And is this not in accord with modern anthropological insights? What once we distinguished as 'body' and 'soul' we now consider one. Man is a unity, not a duality. He is body-soul, or he is nothing. Any credible modern doctrine of life after death must therefore mean another mode of existence for the *whole* man. Is not this precisely what the Christian doctrine of resurrection expresses? Every man will rise again in his own likeness, his own unchangeable individuality, but *not* in the flesh. Nay, is it not what we believe happened to our Lord himself? For when we say that Jesus was raised from the dead – and the apostles say 'he was raised' rather than 'he rose' – we mean that he really slept the sleep of death, that he came to life again – awoke – at God's mighty touch, not as a disembodied spirit but in the fullness of his personality, so that, though different (as on the Emmaus Road) he was still recognizably the same person (whom Thomas was invited to touch) as his disciples had known before the cross.

II

From the risen Christ let us now turn to life in the risen Lord.

For Paul, resurrection is not something that only happens at the End-time. Rather is it something which, by the Holy Spirit's power, begins to happen now for the Christian through his faith-union with the living Christ. In Christ who died and rose again the Christian dies and rises with him into new life now (Rom. 6.4ff.). So Paul can say, 'If any man is in Christ, he is a new creature' (II Cor. 5.17). 'If you then have been raised with Christ, seek the things that are above, where Christ is, seated at the right hand of God' (Col. 3.1). Or, speaking for himself, 'I can do all things in union with him who strengthens me' (Phil. 4.13).

For the apostle the essence of being a Christian lies in this experience of being in living fellowship with the risen Christ – a Christ no longer cramped and constricted as in the days of his flesh but, by his resurrection, let loose in his Father's world to become a ubiquitous and universal personality. And this life in Christ, made possible by the Holy Spirit, is a proleptic sharing in the coming world of resurrection. Though not outwardly visible because hidden under the husk of the old deathly existence, this new life is an *aparchē*, a first-fruits, an *arrabōn*, or first instalment, of the final glory of the End-time.

Physical death, which awaits every man, has for the Christian lost its 'sting' – its significance, because it is no longer the end but only a transitional stage to something yet more glorious. The Christian does not die into nothingness but into Christ and everlasting life. Therefore Paul can say to the Philippians 'For me to die is gain,' since it means 'to be with Christ' (Phil. 1.21-23).

All this accords with Christ's words to Martha in the eleventh chapter of St John's gospel: 'Your brother will rise again' he tells her. It sounds like a conventional word of comfort: 'Remember what our religion teaches about the final resurrection from the dead.' So Martha takes it. But the last day is far away and small consolation to her in her present grief. But Christ's next words startle: 'I *am* the resurrection and the life.' He does not deny the traditional Jewish doctrine. He declares that he, in his own person, is the victory over death, and in him what was a future hope has become a present reality. Then he adds: 'If a man has faith in me, even though he die (physically), he shall come to life.' Why? Because in Christ he has touched the life of God who is immortal. Moreover, 'No one who is alive and has faith in me shall ever die.' Of course he will pay 'the last debt to nature'. But because of that same saving link with Christ – the Christ who dies no more – the physical death he will one day experience loses all reality.

On the doctrine of life in Christ the risen Lord, Paul and John, though their language differs, are at one. Nevertheless, if such life is itself resurrection, it is also a waiting for *the* resurrection. 'If the Spirit of him who raised Jesus from the dead dwells in you,' Paul says, 'he who raised Christ from the dead will give life to your mortal bodies also through his Spirit which dwells in you' (Rom. 8.11).

III

We turn last to I Cor. 15 and Paul's doctrine about the resurrection hope – a doctrine which he says rests four-square on the fact of the risen Christ (I Cor. 15.1-30).

First, however, let us be clear what Paul saw on the Damascus Road when life began anew for him. It was not a Jesus re-animated in his earthly body, a Master resuscitated in his mortal flesh, as Lazarus is said to have been. What Paul saw was a *sōma pneumatikon*, a 'spiritual body', the body of Jesus transfigured by the splendour of another world. This does not admit of any debate. For Paul teaches that a change from a 'natural' (*psychikon*) to a 'spiritual' (*pneumatikon*) body is the God-appointed destiny of the Christian believer;

and since he describes Christ 'as the first-fruits of those who have fallen asleep' (I Cor. 15.20), he quite plainly believed the same wonderful change to have overtaken Christ's body. The 'body of humiliation' had become 'the body of glory' (Phil. 3.21); and in this glorious body the Lord had manifested himself from heaven, where he now was.

Now consider the distinction which Paul draws between *sarx* 'flesh' and *sōma* 'body'. *Sarx* stands for man as doomed to perish, since 'flesh and blood cannot inherit the kingdom of God' (I Cor. 15.50). By contrast, *sōma* is man as destined for God: 'the body is for the Lord, and the Lord for the body' (I Cor. 6.13). *Sōma* signifies the self, the whole man. It is the principle of identity which persists through all changes of our human substance and is the vehicle of immortal life. (Does not this concept of personality accord with our modern psychosomatic thinking?)

Accordingly, Paul goes on to teach that, whereas in this world the *sōma* has a material means of expression, hereafter God will give it a 'spirit' one, an embodiment fit for its celestial *milieu*. The implication is that we shall be renewed not as pale ghosts but with all that is needed for self-expression and communication with others. 'As we have worn the likeness of the man of dust, so shall we wear the likeness of the heavenly man' (I Cor. 15.49). Concerning all this John Baillie[3] has written:

> Paul's hope, then, is for a bodily endowment far more perfect in its organisation, and adapted to a far higher mode of life and a far more intimate mode of intercourse, than any earthly or material body could ever be; and such, it would seem, is still the most reasonable hope for us today.

For Jewish thinking about the last destiny of man, the resurrection of the dead at the End-time connoted entry upon final salvation, the enhancement, not the diminution, of life. This too is part of the Christian hope in Christ. What form this enhancement will take is veiled from us: and, as Niebuhr[4] has said, 'It is unwise for Christians to claim any knowledge of either the furniture of heaven or the temperature of hell, or be too certain about any details of the Kingdom of God in which history is consummated.' All we know is that this enhancement will somehow be recognizable when we enter on it. It will be like nothing so much as awakening from sleep to the light and life of a new and more glorious day (cf. Rev. 21.5).

'We shall all be changed' (by God), Paul tells us (I Cor. 15.51). Yet if resurrection from the dead will involve transformation, it will be (as we have seen) a change in which personal identity is preserved. For the rest, if eye has not seen, nor ear heard, neither has it entered into the heart of man what things God has prepared for those who love him (I Cor. 2.9), no matter. A strong faith is not curious about details. What matters is faith's certitude, born of Christ's resurrection, that 'this perishable must put on the imperishable' (I Cor. 15.33); and what will happen at the general resurrection will be the fulfilment of our present living hope in Christ. This consummation will be nothing less than sharing in the life of the eternal kingdom of God. What happened to Christ on the first Easter Day is pre-view and pledge of all God has in store for those who are 'in Christ' now.

The clue to our Christian Hope is Christ's own resurrection. Not the revivification of the flesh but the resurrection of the body – of man in the fullness of his personality. It is our Christian faith and hope that we fall asleep in death but to awaken at God's mighty touch, and in a better world than this receive from his hand new bodies for living in 'our Father's house'. The last end of our hoping is not (as the Buddhist believes) the cessation of all desire and absorption into the divine essence, but an arising from death's sleep into a quite new existence where earth's sorrows and sins will be no more, and, in the presence of God and his Christ, with the company of all the redeemed, our personalities will find fulfilment and final blessedness. Then all the promises of the Beatitudes will come true. The mourners will be comforted, the pure in heart will see God, and his redeemed children will be for ever at home in their Father's house.

Not Swinburne (from whom we started) but Browning (with whom we end) is the Christian's poet:

On the earth the broken arcs, in the heaven the perfect round.

With him, as we face 'the last enemy', we would 'greet the unseen with a cheer', holding that –

We fall to rise, are baffled to fight better,
Sleep to wake.[5]

NOTES

1. This is but a more philosophical version of the animistic sense of a shadowy survival after death. See John Baillie, *And the Life Everlasting*, 1934, ch. 4.

2. W. Pannenberg, *Jesus – God and Man*, SCM Press and Westminster 1968, pp. 85ff.

3. *And the Life Everlasting*, p. 254. Concerning this concept of personal immorality we will only add that it accords with the mind of Christ. For was not this what he meant when, quoting God's words to Moses, 'I am the God of Abraham, the God of Isaac, and the God of Jacob', he concluded 'God is not the God of the dead but of the living'? (Mark 12.26f.)

4. *The Nature and Destiny of Man*, 1943, vol. II, p. 304.

5. Browning, 'Asoland – Epilogue'.

27

Our Man in Heaven

Hebrews

I

When some of us read the first stanza of Jean Ingelow's noble hymn (*Songs of Praise* 447):

> And didst thou love the race that loved not thee?
> And didst thou take to heaven a human brow?
> Dost plead with man's voice by the marvellous sea?
> Art thou his kinsman now?

we are irresistibly reminded of the Epistle to the Hebrews. In both hymn and epistle are conjoined the doctrines of Christ's true humanity and of his heavenly intercession. Hebrews is dominated by the figure of Jesus the great high priest, compassionate to our frailties because clothed in our nature, who pleads for men 'at the right hand of the Majesty on high' (Heb. 1.13; 8.1). In the hymn the language is less liturgical, but it too insists that he who pleads with man's voice in heaven has taken there a human brow and is our kinsman now.

It is one of the glories of Hebrews that the writer has an appreciation of our Lord's real humanity unsurpassed by any apostolic writer, while at the same time firmly maintaining his true deity. Set Heb. 1.1-4 against Heb. 5.7, and the polarities of his christological thinking become clear: on the one hand, the man who 'in the days of his flesh offered up prayers and supplications to him who was able to save him from death'; on the other, the Son, the universal heir, who radiates God's glory because he bears 'the very stamp of his nature'. Two convictions the writer holds, first, that Christ was bone of our bone and flesh of our flesh, 'learning obedience through what he suffered' (Heb. 5.8), and, second, that in him God himself came down to us, once for all and for ever.

On the realness of our Lord's humanity, therefore, Hebrews and Jean Ingelow are at one, as they agree also that he who now pleads our cause 'before the throne of grace' is now, in the apt phrase of a recent writer, 'Our Man in Heaven'.[1] Nay more, it is precisely because he is the same Jesus now as then that he can serve as our heavenly intercessor. It was because 'he was made like his brothers in every way' (save sin) that he can now be their 'merciful and faithful high priest in the service of God' (2.17). It is the man who has been 'tested in every way as we are' (4.15) who best can 'sympathize with us in our weaknesses' and supply mercy and grace 'in time of need'.

II

The doctrine of Christ's heavenly intercession may have formed part of the earliest apostolic preaching[2], as is suggested by Rom. 8.34: 'who is at God's right hand, and indeed pleads our cause'. Certainly it was part of St John's Christian *credo*: 'Should any man sin, we have one to plead our cause' (AV 'advocate') with the Father, Jesus Christ, and he is 'just' (I John 2.1 NEB). But it is in Hebrews that the doctrine of 'Our Man in Heaven' reaches its finest expression. Through his atoning work completed on the cross, says the writer, Christ's session now at God's right hand is an eternal act of intercession on man's behalf (7.25). (Is this not the real reason why still today Christians conclude their prayers with a 'through Jesus Christ our Lord'?)

Some people find the high 'hieratic' Christology of Hebrews archaic, puzzling and even repellent to their 'low church' principles. They do not take kindly to this 'sacerdotal' conception of the saviour's work which dominates the letter. Yet beyond doubt Hebrews is 'the Epistle of Priesthood', for its main argument, developed fully in chapters 7-9, is that Christ is the ideal high priest who has offered up the ideal sacrifice in the ideal sanctuary, thus opening up 'a new and living way' into the presence of 'the Father of Spirits', where now as our priest-advocate he pleads our cause.

Yet are our 'low church' Christians wholly warranted in their dislike of the 'sacerdotalism' of Hebrews? What is a priest? Is he not basically someone worthy to stand before God, offer spiritual gifts, and pray for others? Is not this precisely what any true minister is called to do? Why should it be offensive to think of Christ as 'Our Man in Heaven' who does this very thing before God as representative of our race? If we will but 'humanize' our concept of Christ's priesthood, why should the doctrine be distasteful to, let us say, the most 'hardshell' Presbyterian?

It was no high Anglican but a plain Presbyterian, Michael Bruce, the Loch Leven poet of genius who died young, who gave the most moving expression to what we have been discussing. Since his verses – a paraphrase of Heb. 4.14ff. – are not known widely outside Scotland, we quote them in full and leave them to make their own impression: [3]

> Where high the heavenly temple stands,
> The house of God not made with hands,
> A great High Priest our nature wears,
> The Guardian of mankind appears.
>
> He who for men their surety stood,
> And poured on earth his precious blood,
> Pursues in heaven his mighty plan,
> The Saviour and the Friend of man.
>
> Though now ascended up on high,
> He bends on earth a brother's eye,
> Partaker of the human name,
> He knows the frailty of our frame.
>
> Our fellow-sufferer yet retains
> A fellow-feeling of our pains,
> And still remembers in the skies
> His tears, his agonies and cries.
>
> In every pang that rends the heart
> The Man of Sorrows had a part;
> He sympathises with our grief
> And to the sufferer sends relief.
>
> With boldness, therefore, at the throne,
> Let us make all our sorrows known,
> And ask the aids of heavenly power
> To help us in the evil hour.

If this is 'sacerdotalism', why the more of it the better! But, all talk of 'priestcraft' aside, do we not need the doctrine of Christ's heavenly intercession as a complement to faith in his redeeming death? Of course, as H. B. Swete[4] warns, we should never picture Christ as a suppliant pleading our cause before a reluctant Deity – Jesus' parable of The Callous Judge (Luke 18.2-8) forbids us to conceive God as some dourly ungracious being who needs to be badgered into compliance. Rather, says Swete, we should think of him as 'a throned Priest King asking what he will from a Father who always hears and grants his request'. Yet would it not be easier for 'the simple believer' to think of Christ as 'Our Man in Heaven' who has opened up for us 'a new and living way to the Father', and who calls on us to follow in the trail which he has himself blazed for men into that Holy of Holies, which is heaven?

We began with Jean Ingelow. With two of the succeeding verses in her hymn let us close:

> O God, O kinsman loved but not enough,
> O Man, with eyes majestic after death,
> Whose feet have toiled along our pathways rough,
> Whose lips drawn human breath:
>
> By that one likeness which is ours and thine,
> By that one nature which doth hold us kin,
> By that high heaven where, sinless, thou dost shine,
> O draw us sinners in.

NOTES

1. Edward Fudge, *Our Man in Heaven* (1973).
2. C. H. Dodd, *The Apostolic Preaching and Its Development*, 1936, Hodder & Stoughton 1963, p. 31.
3. Scottish Paraphrases, *Church Hymnary* (revised) 140.
4. *The Ascended Christ*, 1910, p. 95.

28

The Christian Idea of God
I Peter 1.3

What is God like? With what image shall we best describe the supreme being under whose mysterious providence we spend all our days? For any religion this is the central question.

In the Bible itself you will find many images for God. To one man he is a great king (Ps. 145.1); to another, a great judge (Gen. 18.25); to a third, a great architect (Ps. 8.3); and to a fourth, a great shepherd (Ps. 23.1). Each image doubtless contains some facet of the ultimate truth: God is sovereign, judge, creator, shepherd, all in one. But if we ask, What is the characteristically Christian idea of God, the right answer is that of the apostles: He is 'the God and Father of our Lord Jesus Christ'.

Now, if this is so, God can hardly be the Allah of Mohammed and the Koran. For the God of Islam is not a heavenly Father but someone more like a celestial sultan, a being of inscrutable will and naked power, unqualified by love.

Nor can He be the God of the 'Auld Lichts' in Burns's day, the God who –

sends ane to heaven and ten to Hell
a' for his glory –[1]

for such a God is the awful opposite of the gracious Father whom Christ depicted in his greatest parable.

Even God as defined in *The Shorter Catechism* hardly suggests the Father of Christ:

God is a spirit, infinite, eternal and unchangeable, in his being, wisdom, power, holiness, goodness and truth.

'Infinite, eternal and unchangeable ...' These epithets

suggest God as an ancient Greek philosopher might have described him: boundless, timeless, impassible. This God is static goodness, not outgoing grace. How different from the living God of the Bible whose workshop is history, and who acts in it for us men and our salvation!

If we are to arrive at the Christian idea of God, we must do better than this. Let us begin with a homely tale.

There once was a Scottish schoolboy who, on being told to 'draw something out of his head', produced some strange hieroglyphics on his paper. 'What on earth are you trying to draw?' said the art master peering over his shoulder. 'I'm drawing God,' came the reply. 'But,' said the master, 'nobody is quite sure what God looks like.' Replied the lad, 'They'll ken when I'm finished.'

Without irreverence we may apply this story to Christ himself. When Christ had 'finished' the work God gave him to do, he had shown men all they need to know about him. 'No one has ever seen God,' says St John, 'the only Son, who is in the bosom of the Father, he has made him known' (John 1.18).

Think, first of Christ's teaching, then of the cross, then of the resurrection.

Jesus, the gospels tell us, came into Galilee with the good news that the time foretold by the prophets had come and that the kingdom of God for which men had longed and prayed was now 'upon them' (Mark 1.15). Now, at long last, God was acting in his royal power, in order to visit his people and save them from their sins. But, as you study Jesus' teaching, you find that the king in this dawning kingdom was a Father, the Father whom he himself addressed as Abba (Mark 14.36; Luke 11.2 etc.), the Father in whom, from his boyhood (Luke 2.49) until he hung between two thieves (Luke 23.46), he lived and moved and had his being, the Father whom he made real to his disciples not so much by argument as by his own life, so clear it was to them that this almighty Father was the last reality in his own life and the source of his unique authority.

Yet if in his ministry Jesus revealed God as holy Father to his followers, no less did he reveal him by his death.

For the Father of Christ is the God of Golgotha no less than of Galilee. He is the God of the cross, the God who willed the way of suffering for his well-beloved Son, and gave him up at last for 'the many' (Mark 10.45; Rom. 8.32).

In none of his parables – not even in that of the Prodigal Son (which ought to be re-named 'the Waiting Father') – did he fully reveal God. Jesus did not utter his full purpose – which was also his Father's purpose (John 10.30) – in any word of his. He uttered it in the very last thing he ever did, the end which crowned his work, and of which he cried on the cross, 'It is finished! The work is done!' (John 19.30). The cross was in fact God's great parable acted out in the stuff of history, a parable whose meaning Paul took when he wrote, 'God shows his love for us, in that while we were yet sinners Christ died for us' (Rom. 5.7). This is what was in James Denney's mind when he said he envied the Roman Catholic priest his crucifix: 'I would like to go into every church in the land and, holding up the crucifix, cry "God loves like that!"'

But it is to the first Easter day we must go for the last word on the Father of Christ. The resurrection is the Father's seal on his Son's atoning sacrifice. By this miracle He reveals himself as a God not only of grace but of *power*. And, as the resurrection meant for Christ himself a new and heavenly life, so it carried a like promise for all who were his.

Rightly do our latest theologians (Moltmann, Pannenberg etc.) emphasize the paramount importance of the resurrection. Every book in the New Testament is a resurrection document in the sense that but for belief in the risen Christ it had never been written. Truly did William Manson say, 'The only God the New Testament knows anything about is the God of the Resurrection.'

What then should a Christian believe about God?

First, that He is (in Christ's own words) the 'Father, Lord of heaven and earth' (Matt. 11.25). He is sovereign and in control of his world.

Second, this God is not static goodness but outgoing grace, a grace decisively manifested in the cross.

Third, as is his grace, so also is his power. Stronger than death is his love, and the power which took Christ out of the grave is available for all who are Christ's.

'Fine words,' the sceptics will reply, 'but how can men believe them? Look at all the evils in the world. There cannot be such a God, because, if there were, his heart must surely break.' We Christians point to the cross and say, 'His heart *does* break.' 'But,' they persist, 'it is God who, as you believe, made the world. It is he who is responsible, and he who must bear the load.' We Christians reply, 'He *does* bear it – look at the cross – and he will go on bearing it till this sinful human race is reconciled to God.' 'But,' say the sceptics finally, 'is not death the everlasting No, striking man down at last and for ever into the dust?' To which, with the apostles, we Christians reply, 'Blessed be the God and Father of our Lord Jesus Christ who has begotten us again to a living hope by the resurrection of Jesus Christ from the dead.' We know that our redeemer lives, and that empty grave is pre-view and pledge of God's final purpose for his creation. Even now, by the energy of God's Holy Spirit, it moves to fulfilment. We may not know what the future holds of marvel or surprise, but we are persuaded that neither life nor death, nor anything in the world or out of it will be able to separate us from God's love to us in Christ. This is the God in whom we believe, and this is the future He has in store for his world.'

Of course, so to put our faith in the God and Father of Christ is not to have all our problems and perplexities at once resolved. Here on earth, as Paul said, we know only in part. Not till, by God's grace, do we stand in the light of his eternity will we have answers to all the questions that now vex us. But in Christ his Son – his life and death and resurrection – God our Father has revealed enough of himself and his purpose to keep us trusting – the mysteries of this world have become mysteries not of darkness but of *light* – and by that light we travel – 'till travelling days are done'.

NOTE

1. 'Holy Willie's Prayer'.

29

The Christian Gentleman
I Peter 2.12, 18

There is blue, says the old proverb, and there is better blue. So there are gentlemen and Christian gentlemen (and of course Christian gentlewomen!). What marks out a Christian gentleman from a non-Christian one?

I

When the ancient Greeks defined a gentleman, they joined together the two Greek words for 'good' – *kalos* and *agathos* – and called him a *kalokagathos*. Between these two words for 'good' we must beware of drawing too nice distinctions; but, basically, *kalos* describes the kind of goodness at once seen to be good (beauty, which the Greeks called 'the flowering of virtue', being the obvious type of such goodness); whereas *agathos* means that which is good in its results.

To illustrate from the Greek New Testament, *kalos* describes the pearl in Christ's parable (Matt. 13.45) for which the merchant sold all he had, in order to acquire it. Its beauty at once proclaimed its excellence to his expert eye. Again, *kalos* describes an action whose 'fine-ness' ought to be immediately plain, like that of the woman in the house at Bethany who poured the precious ointment over Christ's head when the shadow of the cross was descending on his life. 'It is a *fine* thing she has done for me' said Jesus (Mark 14.6 NEB). *Kalos* therefore means 'fine', 'fair' or (as the Scots say) 'braw' and noble in its intent.

On the other hand, *agathos* means 'good' in its effects. A 'good tree' (Matt. 7.17) is one that produces wholesome fruit – shall we say, Cox's Orange Pippins and not sour crab apples? A 'good' employer is one who treats his employees considerately. *Agathos* thus means 'generous', 'considerate', 'kind'.

In the second chapter of I Peter you will find both words for 'good'. In v. 12 Peter says to his readers: 'Let your behaviour be such as even pagans can recognize as good (*kalos*)'. Six verses later, he bids servants obey their masters 'not only when they are kind (*agathos*) and gentle but also when they are overbearing'.

Thus the Greek idea of a gentleman was that of one whose goodness was not only self-evidencing but also, in the result, kind and dependable.

II

When we call somebody 'a Christian gentleman', it is about the highest moral praise we can bestow. The question is, How does Christian goodness differ from Greek goodness?

Go back to Jesus. When the rich young ruler addressed him as 'good master', Jesus at once directed his attention away from himself to his Father. 'None is good but God,' he said, meaning that God is the source of all goodness (Mark 10.18). The first thing about Christian goodness is that it is God-derived, not man-produced. True goodness is not of mere human making, for what man makes is all too often cankered by the sin of pride. Dr Spurgeon (we are told) used to believe that a man in his congregation was the saintliest he had ever met – till the man told him so himself! It is always dangerous to work away at your own goodness – the odds are you will turn out a prig, or a Holy Willie, or a Pharisee like the one in Christ's parable.

Like our modern humanists, the old Greeks regarded goodness as something a man can achieve by his own effort. By contrast, Christian goodness is 'Grace goodness' – the sort which humbly acknowledges, 'By the grace of God I am what I am' (I Cor. 15.10). Somebody has said that a king may make a nobleman, but a gentleman he cannot make. Only the grace of God can make a Christian gentleman.

For a second point, Christian goodness is that which finds its exemplar in Christ, 'the first true gentleman that ever breathed'.[1]

How often in their letters the apostles bid their readers 'copy Christ'! Act as he said, they write, act as he did. More specifically, Paul says: 'Bear one another's burdens and so fulfil the law of Christ' (Gal. 6.2). This 'law' is the pattern for living Christ has given his followers, as you find it, for example, in the Sermon on the Mount. It is *not* a new legal code on keeping of which our salvation depends. What we have in it is a compass, not an ordnance map – direction rather than directions. Yet far more is ours as Christians, for we have a divine Master to help us with the living of it. 'Christ,' said T. W. Manson[2], 'has still two hands, one to point the way, the other held out to help us along.' And, as we set out on our journey, we are assured that he is with us 'to the end of time' (Matt. 28.20).

Finally, in the New Testament's view, the sign and token of the Christian gentleman is *agapē*, that Greek word for self-spending, sacrificial love which is best rendered into English by the word 'caring' – caring for others because God has cared for us in Christ.

The pages of Christian history are lustred with the names of men and women who have shown such *agapē*. But it finds no better modern illustration than in the story of Maximilian Kolbe, the Saint of Auschwitz.

Maximilian was a Polish Franciscan monk whom the Nazis imprisoned in that notorious concentration camp because he had sheltered Jews. When, one day, a prisoner escaped, the SS ordered reprisals. Ten men were chosen at random and sentenced to die in the hunger cell. One was a Polish sergeant, a married man with two sons. As the guards led them away, Maximilian, explaining that he was a priest, said to the German commandant, 'I want to take that man's place'. So he was marched away. As one by one his fellow prisoners starved to death, Maximilian remained lucid, prayed with them, and did all he could to ease their lot. At last, the Nazis sent in a doctor to kill them all, by injection. The last to die was Maximilian. Smilingly he offered his arm to the doctor. That, it seems to me, was the supreme mark of a Christian gentleman. 'Greater love has no man than this,' said Maximilian's Lord, 'that a man lay down his life for his friends' (John 15.13). 'Truly I say to you, inasmuch as you did it to one of the least of these my brethren, you did it to me' (Matt. 25.40).

NOTES

1. Thomas Dekker.
2. *Ethics and the Gospel*, SCM Press 1960, p. 68.

30

Apostles' Creed
and Apostles' Gospel

Long, long ago men believed that the twelve apostles actually got together to produce the Apostles' Creed, each apostle contributing an article. It was a pious legend which died with the advent of the new learning at the Renascence. We now know that in its present form the Creed cannot be earlier than the fourth century. Moreover, at the turn of this century, biblical scholars, pre-occupied with the varieties of New Testament religion, denied that there was any such common datum of faith in the apostolic age.

But as biblical science progressed in the twentieth century 'the whirligig of time' brought in its revenges. With the decline of the mainly analytic approach to the New Testament favoured by the Liberal scholars, and the rise of a synthetic one which stressed the deep unity underlying the New Testament's diversities, all was changed.[1]

In this essay by studying (1) the apostles' gospel and (2) the early confessions of faith in the New Testament, we propose to show that the Apostles' Creed stems directly from the apostles' gospel and may justly be called 'apostolic'.

I   The Apostles' Gospel

In the beginning was the *kērygma*. A generation and more before the written gospels appeared, the apostles were preaching the *kērygma*. *Kēryx* is Greek for 'herald', as *kēryssein* is the Greek verb to 'proclaim'. And that rugged word *kērygma*, derived from it, denotes not so much the action of the proclaimer as his proclamation, his message. It is a synonym for gospel (*euaggelion*), the good news of God's coming into the world in Christ.

Thanks to modern scholars, notably C. H. Dodd in his book *The Apostolic Preaching* (1936), we can reconstruct the apostles' *kērygma* in outline. For this purpose we have two sources at our disposal: (1) the six speeches in Acts 1-13, five ascribed to Peter and one to Paul, which, if they do not preserve the actual words of the apostles, preserve very early Christian tradition, a tradition which bears the marks of having existed originally in Aramaic. (2) Our second source is formed by the pre-Pauline elements in Paul's letters, i.e., passages like I Cor. 11.23ff. and 15.3ff. where Paul expressly tells us that what he says is Christian tradition which he has 'received', or verses whose style and content show that Paul is echoing common doctrine in the primitive church (e.g., Rom. 1.3f.; 4.24f.; 10.3f.). By collating these two sources we may confidently say that the *kērygma* must have run somewhat as follows:

> The prophecies are fulfilled and God's New Age has begun.
> The Messiah has come.
> He is Jesus of Nazareth who, as God's Servant Son,
> Went about doing good and healing by God's power,
> Died for men's sins according to the scriptures,
> Was raised by God on the third day,
> Is now exalted to God's right hand,
> And will come in glory for judgment.
> Therefore let all who hear repent, believe and be baptized for the forgiveness of their sins and the gift of the Holy Spirit.

Whether they spoke of preaching the kingdom of God or of preaching Christ, such was the burden of the apostles' gospel.

Now the interesting thing is that the pattern of this gospel can be traced through all the chief books of the New Testament. Like a song which keeps sounding in our heads in all kinds of circumstances, we can hear the authentic notes of the *kērygma* ring out in gospel, epistle, homily and Apocalypse. There is a story told of John McNeill, the Scottish evangelist, that being asked if he never took John 3.16 as his text, replied, 'Na, na! I have *that* in every sermon I preach.' So it is with the writers of the New Testament. Though they may never consciously allude to the apostolic *kērygma*, it is there all the time in their apostolic subconsciousness, and again and again, if we have ears to hear, echoes and resounds in what they say and write.

The earliest gospel, Mark, is simply expanded *kērygma*; but so also with their own variations, are the other three. All are '*kērygma*-built', preserve its framework, reflect its pattern. The same message provides the groundwork of Paul's proclamation. You may hear the characteristic notes of the *kērygma* sounding through the priestly theology of Hebrews. It is clearly traceable in I Peter and I John. It is to be found in the visions and hymns of Revelation. Thus through the whole variegated fabric of the New Testament runs the gold thread of the *kērygma*. In the apostolic age there may have been no universal theological formula, but there was a common preached message of salvation, the *kērygma* about Christ. Its centre – its diamond pivot on which all turns – is of course his saving death and resurrection – 'delivered to death for our misdeeds and raised to life to justify us' (Rom. 4.25) – but its implied plan of salvation has three stages: (1) the preparation for it in prophecy; (2) the work of Christ, and (3) the fruits of salvation from the gift of the Holy Spirit to full redemption at Christ's coming in glory. Moreover, these three stages may easily be connected with the three Persons of the Trinity, the Father who creates and rules, the Son who saves, and the Spirit who sanctifies.

This is what in fact happened in the next two or three centuries. The *kērygma* about Christ which we have traced through the New Testament, lived on in the church and found its avatar in the Apostles' Creed. For what is the second main article of that Creed but an enlarged and re-vised version of the *kērygma*—

I believe ...
> in Jesus Christ his only Son our Lord
> Who was conceived by the Holy Ghost;
> Born of the Virgin Mary;
> Suffered under Pontius Pilate;
> Was crucified, dead and buried;
> He descended into hell;
> The third day he rose again from the dead;
> He ascended into heaven;
> And sitteth at the right hand of God the Father Almighty;
> From thence he shall come to judge the quick and the dead.

Absent is the emphasis on the fulfilment of prophecy which was the first item in the apostles' *kērygma*. The creed-makers have inserted a reference to the Virgin Birth which apparently did not figure in the *kērygma*, as also a reference to the descent into Hades. (This last had no place in the old Roman Creed, *c.* AD 150, which was a precursor of the Apostles' Creed.) But basically what we find in the Apostles' Creed is the gospel which the apostles preached.

II   Confessions of Faith

But the New Testament contains something else, going back to apostolic times, which, together with the *kērygma*, prepared the way for the Apostles' Creed.

In recent times scholars like Oscar Cullmann, by the use of form criticism, have shed much light on the early Christian confessions of faith. By these are meant the formulas, often short and sounding like slogans, in which the early Christians proclaimed their faith, whether at baptism or at worship or in encounter with pagans. Shortest and earliest was the confession 'Jesus is Lord' (Rom. 10.9; I Cor. 12.3; Phil. 2.11). The title *Kyrios*, it is worth remarking, presupposes belief in the Father who raised Jesus from the dead, as also in the Spirit whose outpouring among men implied that Jesus was now enthroned with the Father (Luke 24.49).

Sometimes these confessions of faith were bipartite – mentioned only Father and Son. Thus, in combating idolatry, Paul declares, 'For us there is one God, the Father, from whom are all things and for whom we exist, and one Lord, Jesus Christ, through whom are all things and through whom we exist' (I Cor. 8.6); beside which we may set I Tim. 2.5: 'There is one God, and there is one mediator, the man Christ Jesus, who gave himself as a ransom for all.' Bipartite also is St John's confessional criterion of Christian orthodoxy (aimed at the docetists): 'Every spirit which confesses that Jesus Christ has come in the flesh is of God' (I John 4.2). But confessional also is the doxology quoted by both Paul and Peter: 'Blessed be the God and Father of our Lord Jesus Christ!' (II Cor. 1.3 etc.; I Peter 1.3).

Yet this is not all. Because the first Christians could not express all that they meant by the word 'God', it was inevitable that bipartite confessions should grow into tripartite ones, like the form of the Apostles' Creed. Confessions with such a trinitarian ring of intention include the liturgical blessing, 'The grace of the Lord Jesus Christ, and the love of God, and the fellowship of the Holy Spirit be with you all' (II Cor. 13.14); the baptismal formula at the end of St Matthew's gospel (Matt. 28.19), Paul's prelude to his discussion of 'spiritual gifts': 'There are varieties of gifts but the same Spirit, varieties of service but the same Lord, varieties of working but the same God who inspires them all' (I Cor. 12.4f.); and Peter's opening address to his readers: 'Chosen and destined by God the Father, and sanctified by the Spirit, for obedience to Jesus Christ, and sprinkling by his blood' (I Peter 1.2; cf. Eph. 4.4-6).

This nascent trinitarian confession of faith was both logical and chronological: logical, because, if a Christian wished to express his faith in the totality of the divine name, he naturally set the Father before the Son, as the one who sent him, and the Spirit after the Son, as the one sent by the ascended Christ to continue his saving work in men; and chronological, because the order in this confession of faith is the order of God's intervenings – creating, saving, sanctifying – in the story of our redemption. It is this faith, steeped in history, which the trinitarian formula expresses. By taking it as the framework of what came to be called 'the Apostles' Creed', the creed-makers of the second and third centuries faithfully preserved the testimony of the first apostles. What in fact they did, as we have seen, was to fit the *kērygma* about Christ after the mention of the Second Person.

We have therefore very good reason for holding that, though the Apostles' Creed is not earlier than the fourth century, it is truly apostolic because it descends in direct line from the proclamations and confessions of the first Christians.

All this should be a warning to Christians who want to repudiate the Apostles' Creed, which is at once the oldest and most widely used in Christendom today.

Some of us may think that it is hardly the ideal form of words for a modern Christian's confession of his faith. Yet even though we may construe this or that statement in it differently from the men who made it, we ought to be able to accept the truth to which it points.[2] Provided we adhere to the *intention* behind such statements, there is no reason why we should not repeat it in church without loss of sincerity or intellectual integrity. And let us remember when we do so that we are not merely making an individual confession of our faith; we are joining ourselves with all Christians, both in the church militant on earth and in the church triumphant in heaven.

NOTES

1. See my *Unity of the New Testament*, SCM Press 1943.
2. To take one example, the statement 'He descended into hell' is, in our judgment, best interpreted in terms of Christ's dereliction on the cross (Mark 15.34) and his full bearing of the fruits of our sin as our representative.